Boss Like God

A Blueprint for Elite
Workplace Performance

K. Lynn Lewis
and Beau McBeth

KL²

ISBN-13: 978-0-9994155-1-1 (Hardback)

Cover:
- Handshake photo by Wendy K. Lewis.
- Blueprint image © Uladzimir/Adobe Stock File #85835050.
- Beau McBeth author photo © Mike Krodel.
- Composite design by K. Lynn Lewis.

Published by KL²
Sugar Land, Texas

DEDICATION

To the Supreme Boss,
from whom we have derived
insights highlighted in this book.

To those whose divine and human relationships
have helped enlighten, instruct, and shape us.

To our wives, Wendy and Erica, and to family
and friends who encouraged and supported us.

Contents

Preface

When Fujiwara Mahito established the hot springs resort hotel Nisiyama Onsen Keiunkan in Yamanashi, Japan in the year 705 AD, he began what is now the oldest continually running hotel in the world according to Guinness World Records.[1] The 37-room retreat's secluded location deep in the Kai mountain region and mineral springs "sourced from the chasm of the Earth, Fossa Magna" has certainly played a key role in consistently attracting myriad travelers from near and far for centuries.

Additionally, the resort boasts the continuity of 50 generations of family ownership and the consistency of a multigenerational staff operating with a shared vision to "embody the unchanging hospitality of the heart of Japanese harmony for all of our guests."[2] Together, these characteristics help qualify this 1300-plus year-old business as not just one of the oldest but one of the most consistently managed leadership ventures currently in operation.

---

[1] GuinnessWorldRecords.com.

[2] Quotes excerpted from the hotel's website, Keiunkan.co.jp.

Although Mahito most likely never imagined the longevity of his enterprise, his original vision remains intact. Perhaps he instituted a superb 5-year strategic plan cycle that firmly established and perpetuated the resort, or maybe he did have a 50-year, 100-year, or 500-year plan. But how many leaders have a 1000-year plan? Who even thinks that far ahead?

A 2016 study of non-profit leaders reported that nearly 50% of non-profit organizations surveyed were operating without any knowledge of or access to a strategic plan.

"The stakes are high," notes Concord Leadership Group founder and report author, Marc A. Pittman. "Nonprofits manage the third largest workforce in the United States, control more than $3 trillion in assets...conserve...care...provide...(and) are a safety net to millions."[3]

> *How many leaders have a 1000-year plan?*

Businesses statistics indicate that approximately 80% of new businesses survive their first year, 50% survive four years, 30% survive 10 years,[4] 10% survive 50 years,[5] and only a few last for hundreds or more years.[6]

But, what about the rest? Why do as many as half of new businesses fail within four or so years, and most organizations disappear before their 10-year, 50-year, and certainly 1000-year anniversary?

---

[3] "Non-Profit Leadership Report 2016," Marc A. Pittman, Concord Leadership Group, ConcordLeadershipGroup.com.

[4] U.S. Small Business Administration, Small Business Facts and Infographics, Startup Rates and Firm Age (based on 2012 Business Dynamic Statistics, U. S. Census Bureau), SBA.gov.

[5] "Fortune 500 firms 1955 v. 2016: Only 12% remain, thanks to the creative destruction that fuels economic prosperity," Mark J. Perry, 13 December 2016, AEIdeas, aei.org.

[6] "How 16 Of The Oldest Companies On Earth Have Been Making Money For Centuries," Drake Baer, 1 August 2014, BusinessInsider.com.

Research has revealed that poor leadership contributes to obstacles, decline, and failure.[7] Dysfunctional leadership is considered so central to organizational ruin that one consultant has stated, "Businesses don't fail. People do."[8]

So, how do effective bosses and managers gain executive competence and nurture healthy, long-lasting organizations? We know that many executives from among an estimated 30 million businesses operating in the United States[9] engage in leadership activities and learning annually. Hundreds of thousands of people currently managing or aspiring to management enroll in Master of Business Administration (MBA) programs every year, making the MBA the most popular post-graduate degree in the United States.[10] And, an online Internet search for "leadership and management books" has yielded more than 130,000 results.[11]

That is a lot of businesses, bosses, and books.

However, which is best? If you could learn from the preeminent expert, the ultimate leadership and management guru, whom would you select? If you could enroll in the best MBA program, which would you choose? If you could study the best leadership book, which would you pick? Where would you turn for help developing an annual and/or multi-millennial plan and key insights from a prominent leader who is a master of administration, people, organizations, and strategic planning?

---

[7] "Why Some Startups Succeed (and Why Most Fail)," Patrick Henry, 18 February 2017, Entrepreneur.com.

[8] "Businesses Don't Fail - Leaders Do," Mike Myatt, 12 January 2012, Forbes.com.

[9] "Frequently Asked Questions," SBA Office of Advocacy, August 2017, SBA.gov.

[10] "Why the MBA has become the most popular master's degree in the U.S.," John A. Byrne, 31 May 2014, Fortune.com.

[11] General search conducted on Amazon.com in October 2017.

With these types of questions in mind, we (the authors) explored leadership and management practices recorded in the Bible[12] to seek insights on how God treated employees. After all, has anyone been around longer, knows people and organizations better, or inspired a more historically influential and popular book?[13]

(*Dr. Lewis*) "The book idea began some years ago. While searching for some pragmatic, biblically-based leadership and management insights, I decided to survey the Bible from the perspective of God as a boss and Jesus as a coach. I organized my results into a helpful framework and invited some local business leaders to four *Boss Like God* seminars in 2013 based on a review of the Old Testament, and then offered another series of seminars in 2014 based on a review of the Gospels and Acts in the New Testament.

Where would you turn for help developing an annual and/or multi-millennial plan and key insights from a prominent leader who is a master of administration, people, organizations, and strategic planning?

My co-author, Beau McBeth, attended both series of seminars and began exploring and field-testing the concepts himself in various organizations and study groups to see if the insights made any difference in his workplace."

---

[12] Research texts included books in the Jewish scriptures known as the Hebrew Bible, or Tanakh, and corresponding to the portion of the Christian Bible traditionally known as the "Old Testament."

[13] In the last 50 years, the Bible sold 3.9 billion copies, "Quotations from the Works of Mao Tse-tung" sold 820 million, and "Harry Potter" sold 400 million. See "10 Most Read Books In The World," James Chapman, 20 March 2015, HubPages.com. Also see GuinnessWorldRecords.com.

(*Mr. McBeth*) "My life personally changed forever through the *Boss Like God* and *Coach Like Jesus* series. At the time, I served in leadership in a global organization that at one point laid off more than 32,000 employees. The insights I learned radically transformed my thinking and helped me improve my management practices. Others joined me in studying and implementing these insights, too, and as our learning network has continued to expand, many people and groups have reported experiencing vital transformation."

This contemporary, extensive review of employer and employee accounts recorded in the Old Testament books of the Bible summarizes numerous practical insights related to our own studies and experiences, as well as those of others.

Specifically, *Boss Like God* explores how the Supreme CEO hired employees, managed them, fired some, and helped leaders and organizations execute transitions in leadership.

Historical accounts and modern examples from various industry fields help contemporize these insights and provide blueprints that can help readers become exemplary bosses and, hopefully, ultimately hear these words from the Boss of all bosses[14]:

> *"Well done, good and faithful servant!*
> *You have been faithful with a few things;*
> *I will put you in charge of many things.*
> *Come and share your master's happiness!"*[15]

---

[14] Deuteronomy 10:17, "For the Lord your God is God of gods and Lord of lords, the great God" and Revelation 17:14, "He is Lord of lords and King of kings."

[15] Jesus, as recorded in Matthew 25:21 and 23.

Ways this book can help

- *Bosses/Managers* – Learn ways to help you, your employees, and organization become more successful.

- *Employees* – Learn what to expect from a boss, how to become an exceptional boss if the opportunity arises, and keys to helping your boss(es) and others become successful along the way.

- *Sole Proprietors* – Learn insights on better managing yourself and improve your interactions with others.

> *How did God hire, manage, fire, and transition employees?*

- *Project Managers* – Learn ways to enhance your collaborations with others.

- *Study group leaders* – Use as a guide to explore and test these concepts in real-life applications.

Design and Resources

- *Authorship* – For brevity and convenience, stories by Dr. Lewis are prefaced with (KLL), and stories by Mr. McBeth with (BDM). Stories by others are referenced either in the text or in footnotes.

- *Naming names* – Publicly recognizable and historical figures are named with actual names often accompanied by textual or footnote references, while some contemporary names are fictionalized and some details altered for confidentiality and illustrative purposes.

- *Repeated references* – The names of some Biblical characters are referred to multiple times throughout this book due to the topical nature of the overall outline. Just like the proverbial blind men each describing an elephant differently, we explore some character accounts repeatedly from different angles to gain fuller and more diverse perspectives.

- *Reflections* – Segments at the end of some chapters offer opportunities for further thought.

- *Study resources* – More content, guided discussion outlines, and other resources are available online at BossLikeGod.com.

- *Coaching, consulting, speaking, and teaching* – Visit BossLikeGod.com for more information.

Join our discussions online and/or
sign-up for our e-newsletter at BossLikeGod.com.

Section One

Hiring Well

1
Introduction

An employer seeking to fill a key administrative position leaned strongly toward selecting one specific contender. A recent college graduate with a respectable degree from a reputable school, the candidate exuded extreme confidence, embraced his handsome looks and engaging personality with humility and aplomb, and enjoyed familial connections with others in the organization.

The employer liked him and considered hiring the candidate without even conducting an interview. However, in deference to the general advisability of due process, he invited the young man to drop by his office for a formal chat.

During their meeting, the prospective employer asked, "Have you ever worked in a similar position before?"

"No."

He smiled. The boss smiled back. Interviews like this were so easy they could be considered cheating.

"Are you familiar with the corporate protocols and management responsibilities associated with this position?"

"Not really, at this point, but I can learn."

He held the boss's gaze calmly and confidently.

Without breaking eye contact, the boss continued asking a stream of questions mechanically that mostly all began with "Have you ever...?"

Without flinching in the least the candidate answered "No" to every question.

The boss shifted to an even more basic query, "Do you know how to maintain files and create reports?"

"Sort of."

He continued to exude poise and unflappability and appended his previous answer with, "I am confident that I can learn whatever needs to be learned to do whatever needs to be done. I am a quick study, and my goal is to help make you and this organization successful."

Finally, aiming to secure at least one positive answer, the boss asked, "Can you use a computer and a smartphone?"

"Oh, yes, I can do that."

"Great!" the boss exclaimed. "You're hired!"

How DOES one find and hire the right employee for the right position?

However, within a short season, the boss had to release his new hire because he could not do the job. True to his word, the new employee had no relevant experience that merited his employment in that position. He certainly had integrity, got along well with the rest of the team, and his vivacious presence brightened everyone's day and helped make the office a whole lot of fun, but he practically lacked even the base-level requisite skills for someone serving in his role that were needed to help the company. He proved positively engaging as a person, but negatively effective as an employee hired to perform duties in that position.

4

This section explores six ways God procured employees, and notes ways leaders today can act in similar ways. The concluding chapter additionally considers God's results in hiring. After all, the Supreme Boss must have compiled an impeccable record of accomplishment in hiring perfect people with perfect performance records. Surely, a good boss, especially a God Boss, always hires the best and nothing goes awry, right?

Reflection

Biases and beliefs affect actions. According to the "Ladder of Inference" developed by organizational psychologist, Chris Argyris, and detailed in Peter Senge's *The Fifth Discipline: The Art and Practice of the Learning Organization*,[1] people often process through a somewhat standard flow of thinking when moving from observation to action. The progression includes observing data, selecting data, adding meanings, making assumptions, drawing conclusions, adopting beliefs, and engaging in actions based on those beliefs. In turn, beliefs impact data selection in future interactions in a cause-and-effect pattern described as a "reflexive loop."

In the case outlined in this introduction, a prospective employer communicates with a congenial candidate who has a personal connection to the organization. The boss gathers data about the person's education, professional skills, and potentially relevant experiences, but cherry picks from among the data based on his underlying beliefs and focuses on several positive characteristics to which he clings heartily.

---

[1] "Ladder of Inference" initially developed by organizational psychologist Chris Argyris, and subsequently presented in *The Fifth Discipline: The Art and Practice of the Learning Organization*, Peter M. Senge, Doubleday, 1990, 2006.

In his own mind, the prospective employer ascertains virtue in hiring the person, heavily weights his appealing personality and personal connection over substantive qualifications, concludes that he has seriously vetted the candidacy, and decides to hire him.

But, without intervention and introspection, and because his hire fails, the reflexive loop in his thinking may cause bias against hiring charming people, recent graduates, or prospects with familial connections in the future.

In the pages ahead, examples include one situation where God chooses a perceived obvious candidate (Saul) that many liked based partly on looks, as well as a following instance where God advocates ignoring outward characteristics to focus instead on more inward qualities when making the employee selection (David). The accompanying process of intervention and introspection highlights God's manager's (Samuel) biases and beliefs that need addressing and leads to a better hire the second time around.

2

Create

Creative thinkers pondering custom-designing perfect employees have brought us characters like ambitious scientist Victor Frankenstein's creature who describes himself as "the Adam of your labours" in the novel *Frankenstein; or, The Modern Prometheus* (1818);[1] Geppetto's wooden puppet who dreams of becoming a real boy in the children's novel *The Adventures of Pinocchio* (1883);[2] the NOVA prototype S.A.I.N.T. (Strategic Artificially Intelligent Nuclear Transport) robot Johnny Five who comes alive in the movie *Short Circuit* (1986);[3] artist Jonathan Switcher's perfect creation Emmy who comes to life in the comedy romance movie *Mannequin* (1987);[4] and the android Data who wishes to be more human in various TV and movie *Star Trek* series.[5]

---

[1] "Frankenstein; or, The Modern Prometheus," Mary Shelley; Lackington, Hughes, Harding, Mavor & Jones; 1818.

[2] "The Adventures of Pinocchio," Carlo Collodi, 1883.

[3] *Short Circuit*. Directed by John Badham, TriStar Pictures, 1986.

[4] *Mannequin*. Directed by Michael Gottlieb, Gladden Entertainment, 1987.

[5] *Star Trek: The Next Generation* (TNG), *Star Trek Generations* (1994), *Star Trek: First Contact* (1996), *Star Trek: Insurrection* (1998), and *Star Trek: Nemesis* (2002).

However, unlike these stories, the first two chapters of Genesis describe a boss literally, physically CREATING his very own human employees. God forms, molds, shapes, and breathes life into two similar, but distinctly different, people in His own image – Adam and Eve. Although the text summarizes creations that extend far beyond these humans themselves, note *five categories of essentials* God provided that employers today can similarly provide.

1 *Purpose(s)*
God gave His employees several defined purposes. They were not just "hired" and left to figure out why they were there. Rather, their "contract" included detailed specifics.

> "Be fruitful and increase in number; fill the earth and subdue it. Rule over the fish in the sea and the birds in the sky and over every living creature that moves on the ground" (Genesis 1:28).

The Boss also put them in the Garden of Eden to work it and take care of it (2:15). Thus, they were placed in a specific location to do a specific job, and "managing the plant" entered the lexicon in the very first human job description.

2 *Resources*
The garden in which God put the people included food, specifically "every seed-bearing plant on the face of the whole earth, and every tree that has fruit with seed in it" (1:29). In addition to attractive, tasty food, the Lord provided water and a plethora of other things in the garden that the employees needed to both live and do their job well.

3 *Opportunities*
In addition to purposes and resources, their employer provided opportunities. These even extended to participation in influential and long-lasting leadership decisions, such as the man giving names to all the animals (2:19-20).

4 *Freedoms*
The Boss gave the employees freedom "to eat from any tree in the garden" (2:16). He also stipulated limitations, which are discussed next, but the element of "freedom" offered an incredibly amazing gift with huge possibilities and potential ramifications, both good and bad.

5 *Boundaries*
The employees' great reign of freedom included a clear boundary with a specific corresponding consequence:

> "You must not eat from the tree of the knowledge of good and evil, for when you eat from it you will certainly die" (2:16-17).

How Bosses Can Create

Unlike God, employers do not have the ability to create the perfect employee either from clay, a rib, or "ex nihilo."[6] However, bosses CAN create and provide a lot. Leaders can begin with an idea, gather ingredients of resources and people with talent in the right proportions, place them in a productive environment, and then guide the making, mixing, molding, and processing that results in the creation of beneficial products and/or nourishing services.

---

[6] Latin phrase meaning "out of nothing; from nothing," Dictionary.com.

Make Preparations

After months of onboarding discussions and planning, and a splashy hiring announcement, a boss joyfully welcomed his newest employee and led him to his new office. However, nothing seemed prepared for the employee's arrival.

Another long-term employee already occupied the office and had accumulated files and resources everywhere – on the desk, piled in chairs, over and under the counters, and all over the floor. The old employee planned to remain in the office, and the two employees were slated to share the workspace.

However, no preparations had been made ahead of time to dedicate any obvious space for the new employee's exclusive use. The boss literally walked in and slid some materials over on one of the counters to make some room.

When he realized the office had no chair available for the new employee to sit in, he sent someone else to bring a spare chair from another office. He also noticed the office had no computer, phone, supplies or any other resources prepared or available for the new employee. After making promises to work on it, he left the new officemates alone. For the next few weeks, the new employee slowly accumulated the resources he needed to start the job the boss hired him to do, and he realized early on that the new boss might lack some skills in proactive thinking, forward planning, and attention to the needs of personnel.

Make Adjustments

Just as employees can benefit from a welcoming launch and the initial provision of resources needed to perform their duties, creating employees may also extend to administering critical adjustments along the way.

Adam and Eve initially received clear job descriptions that outlined the purposes, opportunities, resources, freedoms, and boundaries associated with their employment. Although job descriptions do not create success or failure, or control obedience or disobedience, reality and expectations do need defining.

After the couple crossed the forbidden boundary, God followed through on His promises and made corresponding adjustments that essentially re-created their employment circumstances in several ways. He added additional elements to their job description, relocated them to a new environment, and provided additional resources for protection (cherubim and a flaming sword guarding the way to the tree of life) and provision (clothes).

Much like in meal preparation, the best time to adjust a recipe is before an item is cooked. Similarly, bosses may need to make critical early adjustments during the process of "giving life" and stationing new employees.

Reflection

Consider your employees. Review their job descriptions to see if the phrases sufficiently detail their purpose(s), resources, opportunities, freedoms, and boundaries. Make a list of ways you as a boss have helped each employee settle in, succeed, thrive, and grow. Add to the list things you could or maybe should do, such as asking for their input, assigning them to a team or special project, providing a range of opportunities for training, or pairing them with a mentor. You might even request their perspectives on the above, asking "Have I helped you settle in, succeed, thrive, and grow? How exactly? How can I improve?"

Employer Action Item Checklist

1. Review employee job description.

   ___ Purpose(s) ___ Resources ___ Opportunities
   ___ Freedoms ___ Boundaries

2. Personal reflection: How do I believe I have helped the employee settle in, succeed, thrive, grow?

3. Employee interaction: How have I helped you succeed, thrive, and grow? How exactly? How can I improve?

(KLL) During my first year after graduating with a bachelor's degree in Agricultural Engineering from the University of Georgia, I worked as a hydrologist and dam engineer under an older, rival Clemson University graduate who owned his own civil engineering firm and who personally trained me in the design and management of projects from beginning to end.

We pulled books off shelves and looked up hydrologic charts and tables. We performed calculations by hand (he preferred a slide rule, I preferred a calculator). We put pencil to paper and ink to vellum and poured through files and paperwork in the office. We walked and talked over wooded hills and vales, muddy fields, waded and dove in water (I dove, he sat in the boat), sorted through soils, performed perc tests, and visited with owners and builders on-site and agents and agencies in their offices.

> *My* success became
> *his* success became
> *our* success

We also attended local, regional, and national conferences and seminars together. He sent me out into the professional engineering community for hands-on-training in the offices of other engineers and industry professionals. He challenged me with increasingly difficult assignments, patiently guided my journey of learning through trial and error, continually requested my input, and opened doors of opportunity for me through the sharing of his wisdom, his experiences and expertise, and his connections.

In retrospect, I believe he passionately wanted to help me "Be All You Can Be"[7] in the workplace. Under his leadership, I settled in, succeeded, thrived, and grew, and *my* success became *his* success became *our* success because he contributed to helping "create" me. No, he did not literally create me from scratch, but his efforts did transform me from a learner with potential into a budding industry professional. He took a lump of educated but inexperienced clay, shaped me into a useful vessel, and put me through the hardening fires of experience so I could serve a useful purpose.

Although I later moved into full-time careers in ministry, business, and education, Dan McGill's[8] dynamic example, influence, and training helped shape me not only for work in a professional career, but also for life.

---

[7] "Be All You Can Be" entered the lexicon of popular American culture during use of the phrase as a slogan by the U.S. Army for recruitment between 1980 and 2001. Created by one the oldest ad agencies in the nation at the time, N.W. Ayer, the campaign received ranking Number 18 in Advertising Age's December 1999 listing of "the top one hundred campaigns of the 20th Century."

[8] Born in 1935 in Anderson, South Carolina, Dan McClure McGill died in 2013 at his residence in Gainesville, Georgia. He began his career in 1960 working for the USDA Soil Conservation Service, and then founded and managed his own civil engineering practice for decades before retiring from the firm of Schnabel Engineering in 2001. His career included the design and construction management of hundreds of earthen dams throughout the southeastern U.S.

3
Find

In some cases, God FOUND favorable employees. The first instance where Scripture mentions finding describes a situation, like what sometimes happens today, in which an enterprise reached a point where the employees were so corrupt and performing so disappointingly and dangerously that the Boss decided to shut the company down.

"The Lord saw how great the wickedness of the human race had become on the earth, and that every inclination of the thoughts of the human heart was only evil all the time. The Lord regretted that he had made human beings on the earth, and his heart was deeply troubled. So the Lord said, 'I will wipe from the face of the earth the human race I have created—and with them the animals, the birds and the creatures that move along the ground—for I regret that I have made them.' But Noah found favor in the eyes of the Lord" (Genesis 6:5-8).

Amidst all the corruption, one decent person stood out. Noah apparently enjoyed a good reputation and had a relationship with God (Genesis 6:9). The Boss later further specified why Noah appealed to him as a prospective employee, explaining, "I have found you righteous in this generation" (7:1).

Upon finding a favorable candidate, notice that the Boss met with the prospective employee and shared His plan. The plan included a very detailed description of the problem (or, as some would prefer to say, "opportunity"), the proposed solution, and the prospective employee's role in it.

Consider the epic vision casting. Noah gets the scoop on the Master's plan to destroy every living thing on earth, except for a select few preserved via a specially designed ark made of a certain type of wood, coated with pitch inside and out, approximately 450' long, 75' wide, and 45' high, with a door in the side and three levels of decks (visit ArkEncounter.com to see a contemporary rendition of a full-size replica).

The Boss also instructs Noah to prepare enough food for a total of eight people – Noah and his wife, and their three boys and their wives – along with two of every living creature, male and female (Genesis 6:13-21).

Following the finding, vision casting, sharing the job description about what to do, how to do it, and why (Genesis 6:13-21), Noah received the following contract offer, to which he responded by accepting and obeying:

"I will establish my covenant with you, and you will enter the ark — you and your sons and your wife and your sons' wives with you" (Genesis 6:18).

Contemporary Finding

Finding prospects in modern times often includes a basic process of identifying available positions, wording position parameters, advertising openings, and reviewing applicants to determine suitable candidates. Search foci often begin inside an organization and expand outward as needed. Finding often occurs through broad searches, as well as when bosses already personally know or meet someone they decide they would like to hire, or when prospective employees find a company or person for whom they want to work, and they initiate contact.

The employee transition industry is huge. During the twelve months preceding August 2017 the U.S. Department of Labor reported nearly 64 million hires and nearly 62 million separations for a net gain of just over 2 million jobs.[1] These numbers represent the equivalent of the entire population of the states of California and Florida changing jobs every year.[2]

Numerous companies facilitate the seeking and finding. Some primarily help organizations find and vet candidates, some focus more on helping candidates prepare for and discover new employment opportunities, and others do both.

CareerBuilder noted in 2018 that their "global, end-to-end human capital solutions company that helps millions of people find jobs and hundreds of thousands of employers to find, hire and manage the great talent they need" posted an average of 3 million jobs and processed 24 million job applications *per month.*[3]

---

[1] "Job Openings and Labor Turnover – August 2017," Wednesday, 11 October 2017, Economic News Release, BLS.gov.

[2] Calculated using the "Annual Estimates of the Resident Population for the United States, Regions, States, and Puerto Rico: 1 April 2010 to 1 July 2016" (XLSX). United States Census Bureau. Retrieved 9 June 2017.

[3] Hiring.CareerBuilder.com/company/overview, 1 March 2018.

ZipRecruiter – which aims to be the #1 rated job search app and help people find great jobs and help employers build great companies – has reported serving more than 1,000,000 employers and 120 million job seekers in *one year*.[4]

Monster.com notes that their "global online employment solution" has hosted an average of 29 resumes uploaded, 2800 jobs viewed, and 7900 jobs searched *per minute*.[5]

Much finding also happens organically among networks of acquaintances and associates, facilitated by everything from phone calls and emails among family and friends, handwritten notices in storefront windows to postings in newspapers and on social media, as well as position profile packets, video resumes, and schmoozing over meals, in offices, on golf courses, and other places.

The Noah Model

No matter how one finds employees, the biblical model of Noah includes the following action steps:

- Identify a preferred candidate
- Vision cast and share plans
  - Problem (Opportunity)
  - Solution
  - Role(s)
- Provide a detailed job description
- Offer a contract with hopes that the candidate who accepts will do everything as commanded

---

4 ZipRecruiter.com/about, 1 March 2018.
5 Monster.com/about, 1 March 2018.

Generally, the odds of success utilizing The Noah Model prove most favorable when candidates: 1) are righteous, 2) have a good reputation, and 3) share mutual common values.

Reflection

Creating excellent job descriptions and employment contracts can help leaders vet candidates they find, as well as help those found more clearly understand the *Who? What? Where? When? Why?* and *How?* of a job. Such tools help provide a mutually understood framework for assessment *before* a prospect is hired, as well as management *after* a person is hired.

Another relevant factor revealed in the story of Noah is that *single jobs function within a social framework.* In Noah's case, this included his own human family as well as representatives of the entire animal family. Hiring someone and defining employment parameters should include mention of various interrelationships (which in Noah's case included the whole earth), not just references to the employee and boss.

God found Noah and picked him to lead the ark project, but He also picked seven other people and a male and female of every kind of animal to help him. The selection of his own family certainly helped meet some of Noah's critical personal needs, as well as provided practical assistance when he literally needed "all hands on deck." The massive task of finding and communicating with each specially selected animal couple boggles the mind, but it shows that Noah was not the only one hired to do the job. Noah received top billing, but a boatload of others also received clear instructions and obediently answered the call to fulfill their own unique roles in the Boss's overall master plan.

Designing Roles

What about roles? How does one design them? Pat MacMillan offers suggestions for five qualities valuable in helping design job descriptions.[6]

1. *Clear:* Jobs must have role clarity or there will be role confusion. If unfixed, role confusion soon becomes role conflict. Bosses must be clear about roles as an individual employee and as team members.

2. *Complete:* Cover the whole job and associated tasks with no gaps. Synergism is in white space on organizational charts, or in crevasses between roles of jobs.

3. *Compatible:* Match the job to an individual's strengths and skills. Bosses will build high performance teams by enabling time for people to get to know one another, and by inventorying not only the functional skills of each member of the team where jobs reside, but also past experiences, fits, skills, interest, and other dimensions that define compatibility with one job, task, or another.

4. *Complementary:* When designing a role, it is important to configure it in such a way as to make sure that in the process of executing it, the incumbent is not hindering or blocking someone else's attempt to perform their job role.

5. *Consensual:* A job can have complete descriptions and a person's role on a team can meet the above criteria, but frustration can still occur. Bosses should help teams

---

[6] *The Performance Factor*, Pat MacMillan, B&H Publishing Group: Nashville, 2001, p. 88. Used by permission. All rights reserved.

clarify everyone's role, help everyone understand and agree together on their roles, and help strive to balance individual responsibility and mutual accountability.

The benefits of taking this seriously manifest long after a boss finds and selects a qualified candidate. Descriptions and contracts help with onboarding and assimilation into team roles, as well as assessment and possible revision.

(BDM) I once served on a team that included an industry specialist. Several years later while working on a new project, I recalled that this professional had many of the cultural and professional elements we needed on our new team.

He was born and raised in the Middle East, classically educated in the United States, founded and sold several successful businesses, and earned his Executive MBA at one of the top business schools of management in the country. He led a consulting practice at one of the Big Four accounting firms, and skillfully articulated the value of information technology in the Oil & Gas business.

I had personally witnessed him exercising his gifts, passion, abilities, personality, and depth of experiences across strategy, operations, and implementation of complex systems in very difficult onshore/offshore conditions.

As a highly valued asset to his existing team, I expected his current boss to resist supporting a transition to my new team unless I had a compelling justification along with a successor continuity plan.

So, once I identified my preferred candidate, I arranged personal meetings to vision cast and share detailed plans that included the problem (opportunity), solution, and roles of various team members.

I then provided a detailed job description in accordance with God's interaction with Noah and utilizing MacMillan's suggestions, and offered a contract to the candidate – who had already proven himself as a righteous person with a good reputation and shared common values. The contract helped provide a vision with information relative to the opportunity, risks, and rewards ahead for everyone. In addition, the descriptions enabled clarity as to how, when and where the employee's capabilities could align with his calling and integrate effectively with other team roles.

Ultimately, the job description, outline of benefits for our company, our customer, and the individual helped secure a mutual understanding that resulted in both he and his boss agreeing to the transition.

4
Call

G od obviously CALLED people into His employ. In some cases, they seemed to initially lack an understanding of the heavenly caller's identity, and yet stories abound of people responding to summons from on high by answering their perceived call and acting accordingly.

Abram's (Abraham's) call included a relocation invitation to "Go from your country, your people and your father's household to the land I will show you" (Genesis 12:1).

Relocation requests routinely arise in modern American society, especially in business, healthcare, the military, ministry, and politics. The difference is that most people know where they are relocating to, although some military and ministry careers still have some component of "children go where I send you – and you will find out where as soon as we decide to tell you."

Abram received his call at age 75, by today's standards a quite old age to move and embark on a new career in a new location. Part of his call included birthing a new nation, even though he and his wife (Sarah) did not have their first and only child together until he turned age 100 and she turned 90.

Moses received a call from God at age 80, along with a relocation request. Following what turned out to be 40 years of training as a prince in Egypt and 40 years as a shepherd in Midian, Moses met the Supreme Boss in the desert at Horeb, the mountain of God, while stepping aside to explore a strange sight that captured his curiosity. As Moses looked at a seemingly burning bush not consumed by the flames, God called Moses by name and spoke with him (Exodus 3:4).

In Moses' case, God had to explain who He was, what He was doing and why, and what role He wanted Moses to play in the Hebrew nation's relocation. God clearly voiced confidence in Moses, but Moses expressed self-abasing reluctance. God ultimately brokered a compromise, or made a concession, that included a working relationship with Moses' brother in a partnership deal that ultimately lasted 40 years.

Gideon already had a job, too, when God called him to serve in a new position. The angel of the Lord appeared to the young farmer as he hunkered down in a pit secretly threshing wheat in his father's winepress out of sight of the oppressive local tribal warlords. Oddly, the visitor called the hiding man a "mighty warrior," then proceeded to extend an offer to him to save his entire nation, go with him and provide support, as well as give him specific guidance in how to get started.

God also directed Gideon to offer a specific sacrifice that simultaneously defamed the community's local gods, Baal and Asherah. Fearful of his family and the community's reaction if he publicly tore down Baal's altar and used the Asherah pole he cut down for wood to sacrifice one of his father's bulls, "Gideon-the-Mighty-Warrior" obeyed, but fearfully, at night, after everyone except his accomplices had gone to bed. His father, Joash, certainly pleased him when he stood up for him when neighbors complained about Gideon's actions that dishonored their local gods in favor of God (Judges 6).

Samuel received a call from God as a boy (I Samuel 3) and worked for the same employer in essentially the same job his entire life. After his mother expressed her gratitude for the ability to bear children by giving her firstborn son to the Shiloh priest to raise, Samuel grew up in the presence of God and even slept in the tabernacle. At some point early in his life, God called Samuel in a vision, and Eli, a priest, had to teach him how to hear and respond to the voice of God. For the rest of his life, Samuel faithfully lived out his call to serve as priest and prophet for the nation.

Elisha left his respectable job as a wealthy farmer to follow Elijah in service as a priest and prophet. When Elijah arrived to invite his protégé into ministry, he not only found a man so rich that he owned twelve-yoke of oxen, but an owner so industrious that he himself worked in the fields. A leader clearly willing to go all in, Elisha signified his acceptance of Elijah's call by taking the tools of his soon-to-be former trade and literally burning them up and hosting a big send-off party prior to moving into his new position (I Kings 19:15-21).

Making the Call

Calling is a key part of leadership and management. Bosses routinely call specific people at specific times to specific places to specific positions for specific projects.

The work of calling *involves both teams and individuals*. Leaders, like coaches, look at a whole playing field from a game, season, and legacy perspective, while also considering individual positions. Their responsibility includes using situational awareness to determine what needs to be done and who is best suited for the tasks. Calling up appropriate players to fill needed roles is essential, including looking for new people to fill vacancies or new roles.

Calling and leading involves *stringent mental work*. After visiting his father in the office one day, a son commented that he did not understand why his dad seemed so tired after long days at work.

"All you do is call people and talk on the phone all day," he noted. "What's so hard about that?"

Yet, it takes energy for our brains to process 100,000+ chemical reactions per second and 10 billion nerve cells to record sight and sound. The eyes alone work with more than a dozen separate vision centers in our cerebral cortexes. More than 100 million receptor cells in each eye work with four layers of nerve cells in our retinas to process 10 billion calculations per second before an image even reaches our optic nerves.[1]

The complex auditory processing system that transduces mechanical phenomena into electrical impulses to indicate loudness, pitch, distance, and meaning is 1,000 times faster than visual receptor cells. The ear's inner operating parts of less than a cubic inch can distinguish up to 400,000 tone and intensity variations ranging from 20 to 20,000 vibrations per second. Each ear's 12,000 outer hair cells relay information back from the brain, while the 3,500 inner hair cells connect to 35,000 auditory nerve fibers that connect to the brainstem, midbrain, and temporal lobe.[2]

---

[1] "How Much the Eye Tells the Brain," Kristin Koch, Judith McLean, Ronen Segev, Michael A. Freed, Michael J. Berry II, Vijay Balasubramanian, Peter Sterling. Current Biology, Volume 16, Issue 14, p. 1428–1434, 25 July 2006.

[2] "Information about Hearing, Communication, and Understanding - Major Concepts Related to Hearing and Communication," National Institutes of Health

Human brains take up only 2% of our body weight but consume approximately 20% of the body's energy.[3] The energy fuels the body's functioning via electrical impulses that neurons employ to communicate with one another.[4]

A good boss works like a brain works with other parts of the body to help coordinate teamwork. Brains and bosses help others fulfill their roles to effectively function and help the whole organization live a productive life.

Calling additionally requires *executive competence (or acumen)* to help determine what needs accomplishing, by whom, when, where, and how. Sometimes this takes the form of posting an opening, reviewing applicants, interviewing prospects, and eventually deciding whom to hire. Other times it means reviewing a pool of employees and calling someone up for a specific duty. Depending on the organizational model this may happen with varying frequency.

Delta employs a workplace model at some levels that requires calling and assigning employees nearly every day. Ramp Agents, the workers on the ground outside the planes, do everything "under the wing." They guide planes into parking bays, refuel, unload and reload, move baggage to and from the terminal, etc. With more than twenty different vehicles and numerous tasks required, every employee on the team learns how to do everything that needs to be done. This operational model means that everyone available on any shift should know how to do everything that their team needs to

---

(US); Biological Sciences Curriculum Study. Bethesda (MD): National Institutes of Health (US); 2007.

[3] "Does Size Matter—for Brains?" Christof Koch, 1 January 2016, ScientificAmerican.com.

[4] "Why Does the Brain Need So Much Power?" Nikhil Swaminathan, 29 April 2008, ScientificAmerican.com.

accomplish at any time. From among the pool of workers available on a shift, the boss assigns each one to a specific task or sequence of tasks for that period, very much acting like a brain to coordinate and execute productive function.

Lastly, effective calling requires *in-depth knowledge* of an organization, people, positions, and prospective alignments.

Key Elements of Effective Calling

- Teams and individuals

- Stringent mental work

- Executive competence

- In-depth knowledge of:

  o *An organization* – purpose(s), plans, people, problems and prospects.

  o *People* – history, passions, personality, potential, quirks, and skills.

  o *Positions* – tasks, team dynamics and function, technologies and tools, temperaments, and trials.

  o *Prospective alignments* – Matching positions and tasks with people, and vice versa.

Reflection: Am I too old to do a new thing?

- Henry Ford invented the Model T at age 45.
- James Sinegal founded Costco at age 47.
- Gordon Bowker founded Starbucks at age 51.
- Ray Kroc started McDonalds at age 52.
- Ferdinand Porsche founded Porsche at age 56.
- Wally Blume founded Denali Flavors ice cream company at age 57.
- Charles Flint founded IBM at age 61.
- Col. Harland Sanders founded KFC at age 62.
- J.R.R. Tolkien published the first volume of "Lord of the Rings" at age 62.
- Laura Ingalls Wilder published her first "Little House" book at age 65.
- Donald Trump surpassed Ronald Reagan (first inaugurated at age 69) to become the oldest President of the United States at his 2017 inauguration at age 70.
- Cornelius Vanderbilt bought his first railroad at age 70.
- Anna Mary Robertson Moses ("Grandma Moses") started her painting career at age 78.
- Gladys Burrill ran her first Honolulu Marathon in 2004 at age 86 and entered the Guinness Book of World Records as the Oldest Female Marathon Finisher in 2010 at the age of 92.

Of course, Noah wins this entrepreneurial age contest since God seems to have called him to build the ark shortly before he turned 600 years old (Genesis 7:6). So, if you wonder whether God has a new purpose or project for you, your age might not matter as much as you think.

When Mrs. Harold Deane Akins' husband died in 1999 after 61 years of marriage, the 80-year old knew she could have just "sat down on the couch and watched TV."[5] Instead she prayed for a new direction that came in the form of foreign missionary work. Over the next twelve years, until her death in 2011, she embarked on a series of fruitful missionary adventures that took her around the world numerous times.[6]

When asked, "Why?" she replied, "Just because my husband died, am I supposed to sit around and wait to die, too? No! I still have life in me, and I am going to spend it all until I am all spent!"[7]

---

[5] "Christian school cofounder completes memoirs," Dana Clark Felty, 11 March 2007, SavannahNow.com.

[6] "Harold Deane Akins Obituary," 1 June 2011, Savannah Morning News, Legacy.com.

[7] In a 2003 interview with author K. Lynn Lewis for *The Miracle*, a promotional video produced for Savannah Christian Preparatory School.

5
Select

G od SELECTED a new company employee from among a group numerous times.

The First King of Israel

During the formative years of the nation of Israel, patriarchs, prophets, judges and their progeny led the people. Unlike other nations, Israel had no earthly king. They considered God Almighty their Supreme Commander.

However, during the time of the prophet Samuel, the Israelites' envy of other nations along with his own sons' ungodly behavior prompted leaders to confront Samuel and demand a king.

"You are old," they said, "and your sons do not follow your ways; now appoint a king to lead us, such as all the other nations have" (I Samuel 8:5).

When Samuel conveyed their request to God, he also expressed his displeasure. But, God told him not to take it personally since "it is not you they have rejected, but they have rejected me as their king" (8:7).

God noted that the people had been rejecting Him since the day He led them out of Egypt hundreds of years earlier, and shared warnings about the dangers of having a king, which Samuel conveyed. But, the people insisted that they wanted to be like every other nation and have their own king. God relented, instructed Samuel to "listen to them and give them a king" (I Samuel 8:22), and instructed Samuel privately regarding his selection. Then, Samuel met with the chosen man privately and anointed him (9:1-10:8).

When the day came to publicly announce the person selected to serve as the very first king of Israel, all the tribes gathered at Mizpah for the big announcement, sort of like a big reveal with all the applicants present. From among that national group, Samuel chose the tribe of Benjamin. As each tribe came forward, Samuel sorted through them clan by clan and finally chose Matri's clan, and eventually called out the man he had already anointed, Saul son of Kish, as the winner.

Saul hailed from a well-respected, rich family, stood a head taller than anyone else, and seemed an impressive young man. Even so, his hiding among the baggage when Samuel called out his name indicates a less than enthusiastic winner.

When people found him and brought him out, Samuel announced, "Do you see the man the Lord has chosen? There is no one like him among all the people." Then the people shouted, "Long live the king!" (I Samuel 10:24).

The Second King of Israel

Samuel also selected the next king from among a group, but from a smaller pool. Whereas Saul had a private meeting and anointing and then public selection in front of the whole nation, David's selection all occurred privately among family.

The selection followed God's dissatisfaction with Saul after disobedient behavior that dismayed both Samuel and God. Samuel mourned for him, and the Lord was grieved that he had made Saul king over Israel (I Samuel 15:35). However, once God made the decision to fire Saul, He moved on and instructed Samuel to move on, too, and get back to work.

"How long will you mourn for Saul, since I have rejected him as king over Israel? Fill your horn with oil and be on your way; I am sending you to Jesse of Bethlehem. I have chosen one of his sons to be king" (I Samuel 16:1).

Although God identified the family origin of the new king, He did not clarify which son. Samuel embarked on a journey to Bethlehem to meet privately with the family of Jesse. Impressed by the first son, Eliab, Samuel thought surely the good-looking, well-built man must be the new king.

> *Once God made the decision to fire Saul, He moved on and instructed Samuel to move on, too, and get back to work.*

However, the Boss issued a warning to Samuel, "Do not consider his appearance or his height...Man looks at the outward appearance, but the Lord looks at the heart" (I Samuel 16:7).

As Jesse paraded his other sons (job applicants) by Samuel, God did not confirm any of them. Confused, Samuel asked Jesse if any candidates were missing. Sure enough, Jesse admitted the absence of his youngest son due to his shepherding duties. Samuel insisted on waiting while the family summoned the youngster, and after David's arrival, God confirmed to Samuel his choice of David as the new king.

Although depicted as ruddy and handsome, David's rank as youngest son generally made him the least likely candidate to win a position of honor and authority – especially over his own family and certainly not over the nation.

The Prince of Egypt

A more circuitous selection happened in the life of Joseph, the eleventh of twelve brothers, all sons of the original patriarch of the twelve tribes of Israel. Again, the second to the youngest son should have been among the last and least likely candidates to save his family, lead a nation, and inspire an award-winning musical.[1]

Yet, in his dreams, Joseph saw himself as the lead sheaf to whom all others bowed; the one to whom the sun, moon, and eleven stars bowed their heavenly host to in allegiance and honor. Though his father favored him with a richly ornamented robe, his brothers were

> *God guided Joseph in a journey to place him in the right place at the right time for the right reason for a righteous purpose.*

jealous, mean, and hated him enough to want to kill him, but settled for selling him into slavery instead (Genesis 37). The candidate pool's aversion to their brother's leadership waned when his position, provision, and forgiveness saved their lives and provided for their entire family's future. Although they did not select him from among their group, God guided Joseph in a journey to place him in the right place at the right time for the right reason for a righteous purpose.

---

[1] *Joseph and the Amazing Technicolor Dreamcoat*, with music by 20-year old Andrew Lloyd Webber and lyrics by 23-year old Tim Rice was originally staged as 20-minute "pop cantata" at Colet Court School in London on 1 March 1968.

The Queen of Persia

During a party hosted for kingdom leaders by the king of Persia around 483 BC, the Persian king's wife refused to present herself to guests of her husband when he called her. In response to her embarrassing public behavior, King Xerxes decided to seek a new queen. He physically sorted through many candidates over the next four years or so before finally selecting Esther. Each candidate in the harem spent a year in preparation before their "interview," and only returned to the king if they were summoned by name from among all the other concubines afterwards.

A descendant of Jewish exiles living in the Persian capital of Susa – a world away from her family homeland – Esther initially kept her ancestry a secret. She believed that if the king knew her heritage, he would not even consider her as an option. However, Esther so impressed King Xerxes that he did select her to serve as his new Queen. At the same time, God selected and positioned her for His heavenly purposes. From her position and in her role, she helped turn a planned tragedy into a promising triumph for vast numbers of people living in the 127 provinces from India to Cush that lived under control of the Persian kingdom at that time (Esther 1-10).

The Advisor of Babylon

A member of the royal family in Judah, Daniel found himself among a group of healthy, intelligent, young men taken captive around 605 BC by the Babylonian King Nebuchadnezzar and installed in the royal palace in Babylon.

Over three years of training, four of those men stood out as particularly impressive, described as "ten times better than all the magicians and enchanters in the whole kingdom"

(Daniel 1:20). Of the four, Daniel, received the most excellent commendations and proved himself worthy of trust, honor, and the privilege of dispensing wisdom. Like Joseph, who secured an essentially second-in-command role in the foreign nation of Egypt, and Esther, who secured a favored position in the foreign nation of Persia, Daniel's character, spirit, and talent made him one of the Babylonian king's most trusted administrators. Daniel "so distinguished himself...by his exceptional qualities" (6:3) and was so "highly esteemed" (9:23, 10:18) that he received both earthly and heavenly favor.

Bosses Selecting

Some candidates amongst a group seem like obvious choices, but God seems to have a propensity for selecting people who are not clear shoo-ins. Joseph, Esther, and Daniel all rose to leadership among foreigners, yet their inward character, integrity, and spirit uniquely set them apart, along with their apparently pleasing outward looks.

God sometimes selected leaders to serve in positions *outside* of their normal contexts. All the character examples in this chapter essentially served in secular government positions, yet they each played roles in God's larger purposes.

Biblical candidates additionally tended to go through some sort of vetting process. Esther's took a year, Daniel's three years, and Joseph's much longer. God selected Saul, but then Saul earned his kingship by his actions when the nation needed help. God selected David earlier in Saul's reign, but then he endured years of subservience and endangerment under King Saul, perhaps all part of God's way of training and preparing the young shepherd for his own kingship over a more unified kingdom.

Sometimes, people were selected for a position long before they attained the rank and role, meaning that their journeys included seasons of preparation and indicating that perhaps God wants to use us where we are, while also preparing us for where He wants us to be. Consider David:

- While David learned to tend his family's sheep, God prepared him to shepherd a nation.

- While David fought battles for King Saul, God simultaneously trained a warrior king.

> *God wants to use us where we are, while also preparing us for where He wants us to be.*

- While David hid out in exile and on the run, God trained him in understanding the ways of his enemies and secret places within his own country.

- While David learned to vanquish inside and outside opponents and make key alliances, God prepared him to bring the nation to the brink of a consolidated kingdom, which David would then hand over to his successor for a season of unparalleled peace and prosperity.

Providential Preparation

Consider God's providence in preparing the very first President of the United States of America. The only candidate ever selected by the Electoral College with unanimous approval, George Washington worked as a farmer and surveyor and owned one of Virginia's largest estates prior to the age of 20. He then served as an officer in the British army prior to his 1775 appointment as Major General and Commander-in-Chief of the colonial forces against Great

Britain, all of which occurred prior to his election to the presidency of the new American nation in 1789.

While his early education and experiences prepared him for family, estate, and colonial leadership, those combined helped prepare him for military leadership. Then, those combined helped prepare him for entrepreneurial political leadership that helped legitimize the fledgling nation and define the parameters and tone of an admirable presidency.

Washington rarely sought the positions in which he served, but routinely found himself selected for duty – as a farmer, surveyor, landowner, military leader, and then political leader. Friends and enemies alike respected his character and accomplishments. Upon his death, even the English fleet paid him tribute, and Napoleon Bonaparte ordered 10 days of mourning in France.

Washington believed that the Supreme Commander not only prepared and spared him for service, but privileged him to serve along with a company of others, as evidenced in this excerpt from his letter to Lucretia Wilhelmina van Winter dated 30th March 1785,

> *"At best, I have only been an instrument in the hands of Providence to effect, with the aid of France, and many virtuous fellow Citizens of America, a revolution which is interesting to the liberties of Mankind – and to the emancipation of a Country which may afford an asylum (if we are wise enough to pursue the paths which lead to virtue & patriotism) to the oppressed and needy of the Earth."*

Washington's journey of increasingly public selections, along with his appreciation for the magnitude of the role and responsibilities that accompanied his tasks, resulted in the issuance of the following proclamation which continues to annually shape the calendar and character of the United States of America.

New York, 3 October 1789

By the President of the United States of America. a Proclamation.

Whereas it is the duty of all Nations to acknowledge the providence of Almighty God, to obey his will, to be grateful for his benefits, and humbly to implore his protection and favor — and whereas both Houses of Congress have by their joint Committee requested me "to recommend to the People of the United States a day of public thanksgiving and prayer to be observed by acknowledging with grateful hearts the many signal favors of Almighty God especially by affording them an opportunity peaceably to establish a form of government for their safety and happiness."

Now therefore I do recommend and assign Thursday the 26th day of November next to be devoted by the People of these States to the service of that great and glorious Being, who is the beneficent Author of all the good that was, that is, or that will be — That we may then all unite in rendering unto him our sincere and humble thanks — for his kind care and protection of the

People of this Country previous to their becoming a Nation — for the signal and manifold mercies, and the favorable interpositions of his Providence which we experienced in the course and conclusion of the late war — for the great degree of tranquility, union, and plenty, which we have since enjoyed — for the peaceable and rational manner, in which we have been enabled to establish constitutions of government for our safety and happiness, and particularly the national One now lately instituted — for the civil and religious liberty with which we are blessed; and the means we have of acquiring and diffusing useful knowledge; and in general for all the great and various favors which he hath been pleased to confer upon us.

And also that we may then unite in most humbly offering our prayers and supplications to the great Lord and Ruler of Nations and beseech him to pardon our national and other transgressions — to enable us all, whether in public or private stations, to perform our several and relative duties properly and punctually — to render our national government a blessing to all the people, by constantly being a Government of wise, just, and constitutional laws, discreetly and faithfully executed and obeyed — to protect and guide all Sovereigns and Nations (especially such as have shewn kindness onto us) and to bless them with good government, peace, and concord — To promote the knowledge and practice of true religion and virtue, and the increase of science among them and us — and generally to grant unto all Mankind such a degree of temporal prosperity as he alone knows to be best.

Given under my hand at the City of New-York the third day of October in the year of our Lord 1789.

Go: Washington

Reflection

Whether with or without the benefit of divine Providence, vetting candidates usually requires a process of discernment. Especially when bosses have no prior experience with prospects, knowing a person's training, background, and work experiences can help.

Performance-based interviews engage candidates in dialogue to probe core competencies and skills, as well as to determine if and how well a person can articulate them. Questions revolve around the following dimensions.

- Interpersonal Effectiveness
- Customer Service
- Systems Thinking
- Flexibility/Adaptability
- Creative Thinking
- Organizational Stewardship
- Personal Mastery
- Technical Skills

The questions on the next few pages include some sample generalized examples that may be modified to fit specific job situations as warranted.

1. *Interpersonal Effectiveness*
   - Give a specific example of a time you had to deal with an upset co-worker, patient, or other customer.
     - What was the person upset about and how did you handle it?
     - What was the outcome?
   - Part of this job includes documenting your work.
     - Give a specific example of something you had to write for your boss in the past three months.
     - What feedback did you get from your boss?

2. *Customer Service*
   - Tell about a situation at work where you realized a person needed help.
     - How did you realize the person needed assistance and what did you do?
     - What was the outcome of this situation?
   - Tell about a situation where you helped a co-worker.
     - What was the situation?
     - What was your involvement and what was the outcome?
   - Tell about a specific time when you resolved a difficult customer complaint.
     - What did you do?
     - What was the outcome?

3. *Systems Thinking*

- How does the work you are currently doing affect your organization's ability to meet mission and goals?
  - Do you think your work is important?
  - If yes, why? If no, why not?
- Describe a time when you went above and beyond your job description.
  - What motivated you to put forth extra effort?
  - How did you feel when the job was finished?
  - Did others realize you put forth extra effort?
  - What feedback did you get for your effort?
- Describe a time when you had to take on extra responsibilities or make some other sacrifices for an overall improvement in the service of your team to its customers to occur.
  - How did you feel about making the change?
  - What did you say to co-workers and your boss about the change?
  - How do you feel about the change now?
  - Has it produced better service for your customers?

4. *Flexibility/Adaptability*

- Describe any changes in your work you have personally had to make in the last couple of years.
    - How did you feel about making the change then?
    - What did you do to make the change?
    - How do you feel about the change now?
- Share the last new job procedure you had to learn.
    - What specifically was the hardest aspect of learning the new procedure?
    - What specifically did you like best about learning the new procedure?
    - How well is the new procedure working now?

5. *Creative Thinking*

- Name two suggestions that you made to your boss in the past year.
    - How did you come up with the ideas?
    - What happened?
    - How do you feel about the results?
- Describe a specific time when you suggested improvements to the quality of your team's work.
- Describe a specific time when you suggested improvements to the efficiency of your team.

6. *Organizational Stewardship*

- Share a time when you defended your organization.
  - How did you feel about doing it?
  - How did you go about doing it?
  - What was the response of the other party/parties?
- Describe a specific time when people outside your organization criticized it unfairly.
  - What did you do or say?
  - How successful were you in changing minds or attitudes?
  - What evidence suggests that you were successful in your efforts to change their minds?

7. *Personal Mastery*

- Name three things you have done in the past two years to grow in your job.
- Describe a time when you received negative feedback and turned it into something positive.
- What professional development activities are you currently engaged in?
- What has been the most significant learning lately?
  - Have you made any changes to the way you work as a result?
  - What has impacted you in the context of working with your boss and your team?

8. *Technical Skills*

    - Rate yourself on a scale of 0 to 10 with 0 indicating no knowledge or skill, and 10 indicating superior knowledge and skill on the following areas:

        (Provide approximately 10 areas of knowledge or skills specific to job – list skills such as typing, work processing to higher-level, improving skills such as negotiation and conflict resolution, etc.)

    - Give an example of how you have used a technical skill in your field in your current position.

    - Compare what you know about the job for which you are interviewing with your current own knowledge and skill set.

    - What areas of development do you feel you will need to improve upon or acquire to meet job expectations for this job?

6

Anoint

A tendency toward self-centeredness can tempt many to focus primarily on their own team, and interpret others as doing the same thing. For example, when reading the Bible, some commonly think of the Hebrew/Jewish nation of Israel in the Old Testament and Christians in New Testament as God's team, while everyone else is considered as existing outside the realm of God's purview and interest.

However, the Boss makes it clear that the entire world is His, including everything and everyone in it.[1] His purpose for the nation of Israel, and Christians (collectively called "the Church"), included serving as instruments of blessing others.

---

[1] God makes these claims in various places in the Bible, including:

- Exodus 19:5-6, "Although the whole earth is mine, you will be for me a kingdom of priests and a holy nation."
- Deuteronomy 10:14 and 17, "To the Lord your God belong the heavens, even the highest heavens, the earth and everything in it."
- Psalm 24:1, "The earth is the Lord's, and everything in it."
- Psalm 50:10-11, "Every animal of the forest is mine, and the cattle on a thousand hills. I know every bird in the mountains, and the insects in the fields are mine...for the world is mine, and all that is in it."
- Isaiah 66:1-2, "Heaven is my throne, and the earth is my footstool.... Has not my hand made all these things, and so they came into being?"

In his initial call to Abram, God indicated that through Abram's promised son the whole earth would be blessed. Thus, Isaac's specific purpose included serving as a unique avenue of blessing the whole earth (Genesis 12:1-3).

At the same time, God clearly used people who were not Hebrew/Jewish to help accomplish His purposes. He hired, or ANOINTED, outsiders to serve as part of His overall team. In the business world, this is often called "outsourcing."

Cyrus of Persia

Cyrus ruled Persia as a political leader, not a religious leader. However, hundreds of years before he rose to power, the prophet Isaiah called out his name and the name of his nations long before the birth of Cyrus and rise of the Median and Persian kingdoms as world powers.

God calls the future foreign leader "my shepherd" (Isaiah 44:28) and "my anointed" (45:1). Isaiah prophesies that God would summon Cyrus by name (45:4-7), and God did eventually move Cyrus to serve God's purposes (Ezra 1:1).

Isaiah's prophecies are so extraordinarily detailed that doubting scholars insist they must have been written retroactively hundreds of years later and certainly after the life of Cyrus. In contrast, believers point out that there is no evidence to support such claims and that the very nature of a true prophet and real prophecy is whether what a prophet prophesies comes true or not. What Isaiah prophesied about Cyrus did come true, which gave credence for believing Isaiah's prophecies about the Messiah, many of which are claimed to have been fulfilled down to the smallest details in the life and death of Jesus Christ 700 years or so later.

Thus, in serving as prophetic matchmaker, Isaiah showed that the Boss would use an outsider (Cyrus) to help pave the way for the ultimate insider (Jesus). The Persian ruler's policy provided for exiled peoples to return to their homelands. The Jews return allowed the Israelite nation time to rebuild over the next few hundred years in time for the arrival of the prophesied Messiah – the promised Immanuel, which means "God with us,"[2] and explained as the earthly, physical presence and "image of the invisible God"[3] – Jesus Christ, the primary subject of the New Testament.

Nebuchadnezzar

King Nebuchadnezzar served as a political ruler of the kingdom of Babylon, which the Bible often depicts as a nemesis of unholiness. Yet, the Scriptures call him God's servant (Jeremiah 25:8-9), mention that God intended to pay him for his and his nation's labor (Ezekiel 29:19-20), and indicate that some of his deeds glorified God (Daniel 4:28-37).

Enlarging Our Circles

If God used outside contractors, then bossing like God can include hiring from outside the typical boundaries some perceive as their own team. Instead of racking brains and reworking budgets ad infinitum to try to figure out whom within can do what needs to be done, bosses may sometimes

---

[2] Prophesied in Isaiah 8:8, "The Lord will give you a sign: The virgin will conceive and give birth to a son, and will call him Immanuel." Matthew 1:23 claimed the prophecy was fulfilled by the birth of Jesus.

[3] Colossians 1:15-19, "The Son is the image of the invisible God, the firstborn over all creation. By him all things were created, both in heaven and on earth, visible and invisible, whether thrones or dominions or rulers or authorities – all things have been created through him and for him. He is before all things, and in him all things hold together...God was pleased to have all his fullness dwell in him."

need to look outside their own circle for people and/or organizations not necessarily to work *for* them, but to work *with* them to accomplish their purpose(s).

These may be associates, vendors, or outside contractors. They may not be on the payroll and get a W-2 form from one's company, but they can still function as part of a team whether they get a 1099, a payment, a barter exchange, or a thank you for their donation. In some instances, this network of outside contractors can be larger than all of one's own organizational employees combined.

Just as a sole proprietor may work with many others to provide goods or services, a large company may work with thousands of outside people and organizations to accomplish their mission. Though the individual or company may see themselves as the team, the effective team consists of a far larger roster. Astute leaders recognize this and include outside contractors in their organizational considerations, even to the point of officially anointing them for their roles.

The Power of Anointing

Anointing can make or break a company. Brothers Ted and Glen Jackson worked as apprentices for an HVAC company in LaGrange, Georgia for several years. Eventually, they decided to go out on their own, but they had no capital and no contracts to do so. Following a season of planning and exploration, a well-known builder offered a contract to the budding entrepreneurs to install and service all the HVAC equipment in a new, multi-year residential development. Via the "anointing" by a locally respected company, the Jackson brothers launched "Jackson Heating and Air" in 1973 from Ted's house with Mrs. Nan answering the phone.

The Jacksons' company eventually grew enough to buy their former employer's business, continue building a strong enterprise, transfer family leadership to future generations, and continue expanding services to multiple cities and counties in multiple states.[4]

This concept plays out regularly in business, politics, entertainment, and sports. A coach, team, band, company, director, or show promotes a previously unknown person who then catapults to stardom partly due to their anointing.

Consider the case of the prominent evangelist, Rev. Billy Graham, whose February 2018 death at age 99 recalled his decades of historical ministry and worldwide acclaim.

> "We like to think that radio and television made Billy Graham popular," said Duane Gaylord, vice president of Internet evangelism and digital media at BGEA. "Not exactly accurate! It all began with the telegraph."
>
> In 1949, as Mr. Graham preached the Gospel under a tent known as the Canvas Cathedral in Los Angeles, newspaper tycoon William Randolph Hearst inexplicably sent a one-line telegram to his newspaper editors instructing them to put Billy Graham in the spotlight.
>
> Suddenly, the remarkable stories of people being saved in the tent (including Olympic athlete and WWII bombardier Louie Zamperini of *Unbroken*) were splashed across the front pages of newspapers around the country.

---

[4] JacksonAir.com.

"God may have used Mr. Hearst to promote the meetings, as (my wife) Ruth said, but the credit belonged solely to God," Billy Graham wrote in his autobiography *Just As I Am*.

"All I knew was that before it was over, we were on a journey from which there would be no looking back."[5]

Consider the anointing of the fourth season winner of *American Idol* in 2005, when a previously unknown small-town girl from Oklahoma with no formal training in voice or singing exploded onto the music scene to become one of the most successful music artists of any genre of all time. Carrie Underwood earned her success with talent and hard work, but she reached the launch pad toward superstardom with the help of coaching and promotion by a well-known show designed to discover and anoint new stars.[6]

Then there's the fascinating case of the small database management services and website production firm with one employee and that traded for 1 cent a share that exploded in value when well-known media entrepreneur Robert F.X. Sillerman announced on February 11, 2011 that he planned to acquire Gateway Industries to help facilitate interaction between television viewers and shows. The company's stock almost immediately increased by more than 20,000% based on Sillerman's reputation alone.[7]

In all these cases, well-known insiders anointed unknown outsiders for their own purposes in mutually beneficial ways.

---

[5] "After 65 Years, Billy Graham's Message Still Going Viral," Kristy Etheridge, 20 January 2015, BillyGraham.org.

[6] See AmericanIdol.com and CarrieUnderwoodOfficial.com.

[7] "4 Of The Most Shocking Stock Increases and Falls," James Kerin, Investopedia.com.

Reflection

(BDM) I found the biblical insight of looking outside our own circle particularly valuable as I embarked on seeking an outside hire to serve as an integral contributor to a new team I needed to assemble.

The complexity of our organization, the macro-economic conditions of the industry in which our customer operated, along with the specialized skills required of someone who had served in the trenches of organizational design and value engineering, made the task of sourcing the proper individual incredibly difficult. I found myself regularly praying for a miracle under the weight of the need and critical nature of the job. Eventually by divine introduction, a trusted colleague and friend introduced a qualified candidate.

The candidate lived in Oxford, England and had a resume that included academia and the practice of his scientific study in the real world. I journeyed across the pond and engaged in a multi-day interview process. I knew the proverbial trail was hot when he invited me to be a guest at his home and proposed a journey around his town to establish the foundation for our performance-based interview experience together.

However, it was at a quaint restaurant near Trafalgar Square and St. Paul's Cathedral in London where I fully appreciated what I perceived as God's hand in anointing this person for the role on our team.

The depth of engagement, personal transparency, and purposeful mindset to life were mere icing on the cake. The candles were his willingness to take immediate action to go to the Waterstones corner bookstore when I mentioned biblical insights relative to our business. He noted that 40 years had passed since he read the Bible, even though he was an avid reader with a home library that seemed to rival the American Library of Congress.

We embarked on an amazing journey together and shared outstanding accomplishments in the workplace. An exciting personal friendship unfolded and provided many moments for nourishing relationships with others too.

Hiring this outsider proved a wise and worthy decision because we would have missed out on many benefits had we only sought to source from within our organization.

(KLL) In the pioneering days of the Internet, I conducted communications research over a three-year period that involved interviews with more than 1,100 people and 450 organizations in more than forty states. Of those, I tracked 33 organizations ranging in size from a local sole proprietor to international organizations with thousands of employees.[8]

One key research issue revolved around this question, "Who develops and maintains an organization's web site?" Several things became clear in those early days of seeking to understand and figure out how to use the World Wide Web:

1. Developing and maintaining an *engaging* online presence requires someone who understands the appropriate technology and tools.

2. An *effective* presence requires someone who also understands the organization – history, mission, vision, purpose, services, processes, and policies, as well as the audience, clientele, or membership, etc.

---

[8] *Christian Communication in the Twenty-first Century: Patterns and Principles Relative to the Effective Use of Internet-based Communications*, K. Lynn Lewis, Asbury Theological Seminary Dissertations, 2002.

3. Leaders must determine whether 1) and 2) need an *insider*, an *outsider*, or *a combination*, and allocate appropriate resources to make it happen.

As the emerging technology moved from "Novel Toy" to "Nice Tool" to "Core Tool," it suddenly required decisions related to budgeting, marketing, and personnel. Many leaders raised in a paper world did not understand the electronic universe, the lingo, how to integrate the new tool(s) into their business models, how much it cost, the cultural aspects, and more, and yet they had to make decisions. Knowledgeable or not, their anointings of "webmasters" then made or broke thousands of entrepreneurs, including myself, who found themselves similarly caught up in the digital tsunami racing across the analog landscape.

"Who knows anything about this Internet thing?" quickly became "Who can build our web site?" and then "Who can maintain our web site?" and eventually "Who can effectively and efficiently manage our online presence using the appropriate available and emerging platforms and tools?"

The digital revolution added a whole new department of responsibility to bossing, and, with the proliferation of tools and platforms and uses, will continue to require thoughtful attention for the foreseeable future in most industries.

Astute leadership blueprinting includes assessing the utility of others both inside and outside one's own team for mutually beneficial outcomes, making critical decisions based on those assessments, anointing as appropriate, and administering those relationships over time.

7

Appoint

G od clearly APPOINTED people to serve in His employ.
Some might debate whether appointing, anointing, and
selecting are the same, but there are distinctive differences.

Hebrew Tribal Leaders

When Moses received directions to count the Hebrews
shortly after their exodus from Egypt, God gave his CEO the
names of specific individuals He wanted Moses to appoint to
serve as *leaders of the census* for each tribe (Numbers 1:1-5).
Together, these twelve appointees were to assist the nation's
executive leader in carrying out his assignment, as well as
serve as representatives for each tribe, sort of like department
heads or a project council of task force leaders.

Likewise, God gave Moses the names of specific people to
appoint as *leaders of the tribes* (Numbers 2:1-34), sort of like
governors. Essentially, God gave Moses the slate of names,
and then Moses executed God's plan by appointing the
individuals to their positions. The Boss made decisions and
initiated strategic arrangements, while the general manager
implemented and administered under His direction.

Tabernacle Craftsmen

Shortly thereafter in the timeline of their exodus journey, God gave Moses explicitly detailed instructions on an important building project – a tabernacle with furniture and equipment inside, and a fence and other implements outside. The extremely specific instructions related to materials and measurements, as well as the names of persons chosen to lead the construction.

"I have chosen Bezalel," God said, "and I have filled him with the Spirit of God, with skill, ability and knowledge in all kinds of crafts" (Exodus 31:2). In addition, "I have appointed Oholiab, the son of Ahisamach[1]...to help him" (31:6), and have given them the ability to teach others (35:34).

In this case, the Boss not only appointed people by name, He gave them the skill, ability, and knowledge to accomplish the project, AND gave them the ability to teach others.

Interestingly, this is the first time the Bible describes someone as being "filled" with the Spirit of God. Pharaoh did say something similar about Joseph, "Can we find anyone like this man, one in whom is the spirit of God?" (Genesis 41:38).

But, being filled with the Spirit seems generally something that would describe prophets or priests. Yet, a political ruler (Joseph) and a craftsman (Bezalel) – generally both considered secular professions – are the first ones specifically noted for their apparently unusual gifts of indwelling by the Spirit of God.

---

[1] Recent ground-breaking research examining artifacts discovered near ancient Egyptian turquoise mines in the southwestern Sinai Peninsula suggests that Oholiab's father, Ahisamach, may have served as an overseer of minerals, which could certainly have helped prepare his son for helping co-lead other craftsmen in building the tabernacle. See *The World's Oldest Alphabet: Hebrew As the Language of the Proto-consonantal Script*, Douglas Petrovich, Carta Jerusalem, 2017.

The note regarding teaching seems instructive. The ability to teach can itself be a gift; while some may have it, others may not. This means that some people who can do things, and even do them very well, may not also have the gift of teaching. Therefore, asking an expert to teach, who does not also have the ability to teach, might prove a very frustrating experience for both the would-be teacher and student(s).

On the other hand, employing workers gifted in teaching can multiply an educated and trained labor force, and provide a pleasing, productive experience for all involved.

In response to God's instructions, Moses summoned Bezalel, Oholiab, and every skilled person to whom God had given ability and was willing to work (Exodus 36:2). This added information may imply that some people had skills, ability, and knowledge, but lacked the desire to work, while others may have been willing to work but lacked the appropriate skill, ability, and knowledge. Perhaps willing learners can be taught, but unwilling, uncooperative workers – even if they are experts – may not work out so well.

How many of us have known brilliant, incredibly talented people whose laziness sabotaged their prospects for success, while others with lesser abilities find success nevertheless because of their willingness to work hard?

Hence, key characteristics related to hiring well through appointing may include seeking persons with:

- Skill and ability
- Knowledge
- Willingness to work
- The ability to teach, if educating others is a needed skill. Otherwise, this characteristic is irrelevant.

The Ability to See

We might dismissively think to ourselves, "Sure! God in all of His creative excellence and majestic divinity can easily gift others with ability, skills, and knowledge, but I doubt that such abilities are within our realm as humans."

However, bosses do have great power to give to others. Most people gain abilities, skills and knowledge by gifts and opportunities afforded them by family members, friends, teachers, preachers, leaders, coaches, bosses and co-workers. Gifts can shape futures. Opportunities for people to do certain things and go certain places can open worlds that they have never known and that can lead to degrees, careers, and lifetimes of adventures, discoveries, and life-changing actions.

In 1936, Philippe Tailliez gave a friend a pair of swimming goggles. What *Jacques Cousteau* saw when he opened his eyes in the ocean led him to set about designing a device to allow people to breathe underwater so they could see more for longer. Cousteau's amazing and influential career over the next 60 years as undersea explorer, inventor, photographer, filmmaker, and scientist began with that simple gift.[2]

Coaches often positively affect individuals and families for generations through their efforts to help athletes gain and increase in their ability, skills, and knowledge. Coaches can help players more clearly see their own realistic potential.

A small-town boy from Pewaukee, Wisconsin, *J. J. Watt* rose to national prominence in 2011 after his selection as the #11 Overall Pick in the NFL Draft by the Houston Texans. He went on to earn NFL Defensive Player of the Year in 2012, 2014, and 2015, as well as *Sports Illustrated* Sportsperson of the Year in 2017.

---

[2] Jacques Cousteau, Biography.com, NotableBiographies.com.

In a 2016 speech in Port Arthur, Texas, Watt credited a former Texans coach, Wade Phillips, for helping him succeed.

"Wade saw something in me that nobody else saw in me — and that I might not even have seen in myself. But that's the type of man that Wade Phillips is. He leads you to be what you can be, not what you are. He's the man who taught me that my abilities could far exceed anything that my dreams ever imagined, if I was willing to put in the work, if I was willing to listen, if I was willing to play within the system that he's created, and just go out and give it everything I had. So I did. And here I am today, thankful for everything that I've been able to accomplish in my career so far, because of Wade Phillips...Because he helped teach me about the game of football. Because he helped me believe in myself as a player and as a man."[3]

Coaches, including bosses and managers at every level, can help others see things they have never seen before, including new perspectives of themselves. This can happen through appointment to key positions or roles, through the provision of training resources, continuing education, conferences and seminars, gifts of new equipment and tools, and in myriad other ways.

Bosses CAN truly both appoint and gift. In some cases, God Himself may draft an individual by name and call them up through another leader to do something He wants done.

---

[3] Wade Phillips Homecoming Roast, Robert A. Bowers Civic Center, Port Arthur, Texas, 3 June 2016.

Lady with the Lamp

During the 1830's, a young English maiden experienced several "calls from God" that she interpreted as summons to invest her life in reducing human suffering. Though work in nursing seemed a suitable route to her teenage mind to serve both God and people, her family thwarted her attempts to seek nurse's training because they considered such activity inappropriate for a woman of her stature.

After caring for several ailing family members, Florence Nightingale began studying nursing on her own, reading any nursing-related writings she could find, volunteering in medical facilities, informally studying treatments and results, and taking a couple of short two or three-week nursing courses. Despite continued opposition from her family, she received an appointment in 1853 at age 33 as volunteer Superintendent of Nurses at the Institution for the Care of Sick Gentlewomen in Distressed Circumstances in London.

When Britain and France responded in March 1854 to Russia's invasions into areas of the Turkish Ottoman Empire, the British transported their wounded from the fighting in Crimea 300 miles across the Black Sea to just outside of what is now Istanbul, Turkey.

In October 1854, Secretary of War Sir Sidney Herbert reached out to Florence and appointed her to gather some nurses to assist with caring for the 18,000 wounded and dying men trapped in the quarter mile long hallways and deplorable, cholera- and lice-infected rooms at the Barracks Hospital.

Over the next 21 months, Florence and her team of 37 nurses led the caretaking and worked to improve recovery conditions. They instituted a system of triage, improved sanitation and the quality of food and water, washed the soldiers and linens regularly, and Florence personally made so many rounds carrying a lamp throughout the nights that she became known as the "Lady with the Lamp."

Florence Nightingale's perceived initial call from God, and her appointments to serve, led to a lifelong and groundbreaking career that laid the foundation for the philosophy of modern healthcare, transformed nursing into a respectable profession, and improved health standards worldwide. She published over 200 resources on hospital planning and organization that still impact healthcare today, including ward designs, infection control measures, and the championing of a healthy diet. She also identified the need for specialists, invented the pie chart, and inspired the founding of the International Red Cross.

> *Her ability to fulfill (her call and passion) came through persons with perhaps divine and certainly human power and authority appointing her to available opportunities.*

She clearly seems to have derived her call and passion from God, and her ability to fulfill those came through persons with perhaps divine and certainly human power and authority appointing her to available opportunities in organizations where she could faithfully and extraordinarily live them out.[4]

Reflection

Hiring well includes working in partnership with others, including God, to identify and gainfully employ people with the appropriate skills, abilities, and knowledge needed. Some people know themselves and their intended path well enough

---

[4] Florence Nightingale, florence-nightingale.co.uk and BritishHeritage.com.

to pursue proper training and seek fitting opportunities, while others may need assistance in developing and understanding their own potential.

Consider engaging in the following personal evaluation.

- What are my own skills, abilities, and knowledge?

- Do I have the ability to teach?

- On a scale of 0 to 100, with 0 equal to totally lazy and 100 equal to unstoppable, where do I land on the work ethic scale?

- Where would other, unbiased people place me on the work ethic scale?

- Have others helped me succeed by giving me something? Who? What?

- Have I helped others succeed by giving them something? Who? What?

- Are there others I can help? How? When?

8

God's Results in Hiring

A s this section on hiring well concludes, take a moment to consider this question, "What were God's results in hiring?"

If God is perfect, and surely He is, then He only hired the perfect person(s) for the perfect job(s) in the perfect place(s) at the perfect time(s), and certainly every hire He ever made turned out perfectly. Right?

Remember in the very first chapters of the Bible, God's very first human hires for the perfect job in the perfect place at the perfect time did not necessarily turn out so well. In this case, God really did hire perfect people. However, the employees violated a critical term of their contract and caused big problems (addressed specifically in later chapters).

What happened? How could perfection go so awry? Was there some circumstantial caveat in this scenario that makes any sense, that provides any insight, because the original setup seemed perfect?

Yes, there is, and it is part of every hire you or any other boss will ever make.

The ability to self-determine within certain boundaries – to independently choose good or bad, right or wrong, typically called "free will" – introduces elements of uncontrollability.

Even if bosses are perfect, like God, they usually do not control the attitudes and actions of others. Though God surely could, it seems He may choose *not* to control everything. Rather than create puppets or mechanized robots bound to unbreakable code and remote control, God allowed and allows human (and divine) employees the freedom to make choices within certain conditional parameters.

Some people believe that if God really loved people He would not have allowed freedom, especially if that freedom included making harmful choices. However, it seems that true love does allow for certain degrees of self-actualization, even to the extent of self-destruction and harm to others. The history of the world evidences the results of both positive and negative choices in association with the agency of free will.

Certainly, bosses *do* have a responsibility to seek to hire well. However, bosses must recognize that they SHARE accountability with anyone and everyone they ever hire. Just like in the Garden of Eden, everything CAN be perfect – the people, the place, the provisions, the projects, the programs, the pay – but people can still make bad choices no matter what the boss or other employees do.

Sometimes people get in trouble and even fired over making a hire that went bad. But, perhaps more often, bosses and managers punish themselves mentally and emotionally rethinking "How?" and "Why?" and "If only..." While some things may be learned, the truth is that free will can thwart even the best circumstances. No boss – not even God – will prevent some things if free will is part of a hiring deal.

Consider again what happened when Samuel mourned the failure of the first king of Israel, Saul. God picked him, and clearly instructed Samuel to anoint Saul as king. However, once Saul proved himself unworthy through disobedient and dishonorable behavior, God regretted hiring Saul and conveyed his displeasure to Samuel (I Samuel 15:11,35).

Remember that this did not please Samuel at all. "He was angry and cried out to the Lord all night" (15:11), but God told Samuel to quit mourning and go anoint a new king.

The Boss essentially told Samuel, "Get over it, we have new work to do and another hire to make." Just as Samuel responded by moving on in obedience, bosses may need to do the same when a hire becomes too problematic (I Samuel 15-16).

> *Hiring well is a joint venture with shared responsibilities.*

Consider this encouraging message, "For it is God who works in you to will and act according to His good purpose. Do everything without complaining or arguing, so that you may become blameless and pure, children of God without fault in a crooked and depraved generation, in which you shine like stars in the universe" (Philippians 2:13-14).

In seeking to hire well, bosses can pursue a higher purpose than merely filling positions, providing products and/or services, and making money. Additionally, bosses do well to remember that hiring is a joint venture with shared responsibilities between the boss, the person(s) hired, and others, including the Boss of bosses.

Section Two

Managing Well

9
Introduction

Management follows hiring, so this section explores insights relative to successfully leading a workforce, i.e. managing well. The chapters are titled according to various management tasks.

Similar to the number of ways to prepare shrimp Bubba described to Forrest in the movie *Forrest Gump*,[1] these chapters offer a menu of ten diverse categories of what God *provided* His employees, and things bosses can do today to similarly provide for their employees.

The biblical examples show how God demonstrates an engaged awareness of personal and organizational needs, and how a good boss approaches fulfilling those needs to accomplish desired outcomes.

Historical and contemporary accounts provide tangible examples of management in action in accord with noted insights. For example, consider the company surprised by answers to a new question they added to annual employee reviews, "Do you have what you need to do your job?"

---

[1] *Forrest Gump*, Directed by Robert Zemeckis, Paramount Pictures, 1994.

Unexpectedly, leaders discovered that there were often simple things managers either overlooked or failed to provide that employees needed to do their job well, better, or sometimes, even at all. These included small provisions like office tools, a dedicated department copier code, an easier way to scan and send documents, as well as things like updated computer hardware and software, better furniture and filing systems, improved parking, a centralized database, critical training, location swaps, and additional personnel.

In one case, an employee traipsed back and forth between buildings for months simply because an office location (two buildings away!) contained the only network printer available to him. A dismissive manager continually denied requests for a solution until a higher boss stepped in to fix the problem. The senior boss praised the resourceful employee for going to great lengths to do whatever needed to be done to accomplish the assigned tasks and chastised the manager for failure to improve an employee's work environment by solving a simple problem that significantly impacted productivity.

Similarly, the movie *Hidden Figures*[2] depicts a team of female African-American mathematicians who served a vital role in NASA during the early years of the U.S. space program. When the character played by Taraji P. Henson receives a promotion to work in another department in a building across campus, the lack of a "Colored" bathroom in her building forces her to run across campus every time she needs to use the restroom. When her white, male superior – played by actor Kevin Costner – finds out the reason for her prolonged periods of unexplained absences, he takes a crowbar to the

---

[2] *Hidden Figures;* Directed by Theodore Melfi, Jenno Topping, and Pharrell Williams; Twentieth Century Fox, 2016.

bathroom sign, drags it away, and declares the end of bathrooms divided by skin color at NASA. With that roadblock removed, their team helps Americans triumphantly reach the moon and return safely.

Employers play a key role in the staging and production of employee's jobs. From small tasks to outrageous shoot-for-the-moon projects, employers can help their employees and organizations succeed when they are aware of, willing, and able to offer certain provisions people need to get jobs done. As depicted in the pages ahead, God modeled proactive providing, and even evidenced an openness to considering reasonable requests for variance.

> *God modeled proactive providing.*

10

Provide Parameters

G od created job descriptions. He set boundaries, gave directions, clarified expectations, specified guidelines, shared plans, outlined processes, and cast vision. Sometimes all this happened during onboarding, and sometimes during continuance of relationships with His employees.

Adam and Eve received clear parameters (limits and factors) in the beginning. Do this, but do not do that or this will happen. Do be fruitful and multiply. Do rule over the earth, the fish, the birds, and every living creature. Do work the Garden of Eden and take care of it. Do eat plants for food, including eating from any tree in the garden. However, do not eat from the tree of the knowledge of good and evil, for when you do that you will certainly die. Notice the clear parameters, including clear limitations and consequences (Genesis 1-2).

After they disobeyed, God responded by implementing specific immediate and long-term results, including death. God also reset some parameters, including clothing the newly-aware-that-were-naked-couple and moving them away from their first home office to outside the Garden of Eden for their own protection (Genesis 3).

Noah stood out among his peers and received a favorable review from his Boss. This gained him access to an inside scoop on a pending huge deal poised to affect the entire world market. The exclusive proposal offered only to him included an announcement, a market assessment, a specific solution, implementation details, and a group contract. Noah appears to have signed immediately with no modifications or requests for contingencies (Genesis 6).

Later, Noah received praise for his exacting obedience and admirable character, a notification that the promised deal was about to go down, and additional project implementation details (Genesis 7).

As the assignment concluded, the Boss provided closeout instructions and an employee assessment. He also initiated new contracts with the planet, all living creatures, Noah, and his descendants. The revised parameters included a new provision with specific limitations and defined consequences. New provisions included the allowance to eat meat, but with restrictions not to eat meat with blood still in it. Warnings of punishment were also given to both people and animals that killed a human being (Genesis 8-9). Note that parameters the Boss provided to Noah included specific plans and process steps along the way.

Abraham similarly received detailed directions from God over a period of approximately 100 years – the first of which the Bible records when Abram was 75 years old, "Leave your country, your people, and your father's household and go to the land I will show you" (Genesis 12:1). From then on, his Boss provided directions about where to go, what to do and not do, when and why, and even warnings about immediately upcoming and future events.

Moses received direction over a period of forty years, beginning at age 80. The books of Exodus, Numbers, Leviticus, and Deuteronomy provide written accounts of God's interactions with Moses about him, his family, his fellow Hebrews, and neighboring leaders and nations. Numerous parameters are extremely precise, detailing dates, times, weights, measures, colors and materials, people and places, plans and promises. Like a professional engineer, the Boss addressed both the big picture and tiny details.

> *Many interactions depict an engaging relationship between the Boss and bossed, not just a one-way telling but a two-way talking.*

Particularly with Moses, but also with others, there is evidence of a relationship characterized by a sequence of personal interactions that include more than project timelines and data points. Boss and employees share their thoughts, questions, and frustrations, they work together as a team to lead teams, they look for ways to honor one another, they reinforce, strategize, administer, and process loop feedback.

Biblical accounts chronicle God providing parameters to warriors, judges, kings, priests, prophets, and others. Many interactions depict an engaging relationship between the Boss and bossed, not just a one-way telling but a two-way talking as employees speak and work with and on behalf of their boss.

Pressing Issues

A similar daily scene broadcast across the world includes an official representative of the Executive Branch of the United States government interacting with members of the press. Known as the White House Press Secretary, this person serves by appointment of the President of the United States.

"My job is to be a spokesman," explained former White House Press Secretary, Mrs. Dee Dee Myers (1993-94), "for the President, for the White House, to do the daily briefings, to manage the press corps in terms of travel, day-to-day needs, access, interviews, all those issues."[1]

As acting spokesperson for the administration, the role includes unusual advantages and accompanying limitations. The Press Secretary regularly meets with the President, other administration leaders, and members of the press; knows key inside information; and helps shape the presentation of administration messages. However, the Press Secretary does not speak for themselves, the press, or the people, but represents the administration. They are not free to share information whenever or however they feel like it, but must abide by government policy, Presidential and White House preferences, and in accordance with national security.

Although the emotional temperature of press briefings and conferences (usually public and televised) and press gaggles (usually private, but audio recorded) may range from polite to vicious, the clearly defined parameters of the Press Secretary position help the person serving in the role more effectively serve the Administration and the public by interacting appropriately with the intermediary press.

"You serve two masters," recalled former Press Secretary Mr. Ari Fleischer (2001-03). "You serve the president of the United States, and you speak for him. And you serve the press, which means you have a duty to provide them accurate

---

[1] "Press Secretary to an Administration Full of Talkers," Thomas B. Rosenstiel, 20 March 1994, LATimes.com.

information, and to be helpful to them in the daily collection of news. In other words, you're paid every day to walk a tightrope without a safety net."[2]

Myers, the first female in the job, noted that she had different parameters and internal roles as compared to other Press Secretaries. She describes her inexperience coming into the job and limitations that diminished the job included "a lower rank, lower pay."[3]

> *The clearly defined parameters of the Press Secretary position help the person serving in the role more effectively serve the Administration and the public.*

The second female White House Press Secretary, Mrs. Dana Perino (2007-09), described her perspective of the position this way, "When I was at the White House podium, I would imagine President Bush watching me and if I thought he would not be proud of something I was about to say, then I didn't say it."[4]

Perino also maintained an even higher perspective on her job, as evidenced in this silent prayer when entering the White House every morning during her tenure, "Thank you God for this chance to serve the American people. May I remember why I'm here no matter what this day brings."[5]

---

[2] "Careful Steps Took Press Secretary to the White House," Richard W. Stevenson, 22 January 2001, The New York Times, NewYorkTimes.com.

[3] "The Rules According to Dee Dee Myers," Lisa Takeuchi Cullen, 29 February 2008, Time.com.

[4] "Former White House press secretary Dana Perino gets surprise visitor at speaking event: George W. Bush," Julie Fancher, 28 April 2015, DallasNews.com.

[5] "Advice for Sarah Huckabee Sanders from one female press secretary to another," 26 July 2017, Dana Perino, FoxNews.com.

Reflection

From prophets to press secretaries and beyond, clear parameters play a crucial role. Today's global marketplace is empowered by advanced technology and complex systems, with some bosses leading teams dispersed worldwide, in different time zones, cultures, and geopolitical constructs.

For example, Airbnb's first Chief Operating Officer, Belinda Johnson, noted during her first week on the job in February 2018 that their company included "more than 4,000 employees, with teams in 18 markets around the globe overseeing more than 4 million listings in more than 65,000 cities and 191 countries. That's more listings than the top five hotel chains combined have rooms."[6]

Expanding supply and demand phenomenon have resulted in the establishment of these type of highly matrixed organizations serving customers, competing for resources, maintaining a profit, building brand identity, and expanding influence. The sheer scope and complexity of relationships integrating across teams means that clear parameters become even more crucial to helping people work together to achieve market demands for exceptional levels of performance.

"Big software projects are built by giant human systems, and giant human systems run on relationships," writes Alex Hinrichs, retired Partner Group Program Manager for HoloLens at Microsoft. "Bring clarity to chaos, and then write it down. It's difficult, time consuming, requires lots of face-to-face time, and often needs re-working, but it's the way teams make progress with confidence."[7]

---

[6] "As Airbnb's First COO, Here's My Plan," Belinda Johnson, 5 February 2018, LinkedIn.com.

[7] "The 11 most important lessons I learned during my 22 years at Microsoft," Alex Hinrichs, 5 February 2018, LinkedIn.com.

Teamwork is built into the fabric of society. Like a mosaic of different colored threads and varying patterns, parameters help individuals find their place within a group and guide the performance of groups as they work together.

In *The Performance Factor*,[8] Pat MacMillan outlines six characteristics critical for high performance teams:

1. Common Purpose
2. Crystal Clear Roles
3. Accepted Leadership
4. Effective Processes
5. Solid Relationships
6. Excellent Communication

Helpful parameters bosses should detail include:

- Vision
- Guidelines
- Strategic plans
- Methods and Processes – Who? What? When? Where? Why? and How?
- Directions – Clear, Concise, Direct, Ongoing, and Timely

---

[8] *The Performance Factor*, Pat MacMillan, B&H Publishing Group: Nashville, 2001, p. 39. Used by permission. All rights reserved.

11
Provide Payment

E mployees generally expect payment in return for labor, and employers generally provide compensation. However, defining a mutually agreeable fair wage in exchange for services rendered, as well as coming to amenable terms on employment issues, has proven repeatedly problematic.

The first labor strike in recorded history appears in an account of ancient state-employed artisans living in Deir el-Medina, Egypt in the 12th century BC. After weeks of waiting for promised deliveries of wheat and barley wages, the workers put down their tools and marched in protest shouting "We are hungry!" They then staged a sit-in outside the funerary temples of Thutmose III and Ramesses II, and eventually blocked access to the Valley of the Kings. The scribe Amennakht records their complaint, "It is because of hunger and because of thirst that we came here. There is no clothing, no ointment, no fish, no vegetables. Send to Pharaoh...that sustenance may be made for us."[1]

---

[1] "The First Labor Strike in History," Joshua J. Mark, Ancient History Encyclopedia, Ancient.eu.

Since then, miners, artisans, factory workers, railroad workers, air traffic controllers, actors, athletes, garbage collectors, teachers, writers, and many more have staged similar protests related to unacceptable or untimely wages and undesirable working conditions, and accounts of injustice or perceived injustice instigating arguments, rebellions, strikes, revolts, and revolutions fill world history.

The infamous New York newsboys strike of 1899 that inspired the Disney movie *Newsies* (1992)[2] and Tony Award®-winning Broadway musical *Newsies The Musical* (2012-14)[3] started over a difference of opinion between 10 cents. In the days before child labor laws, newspapers were mostly distributed on street corners by boys (and some girls) as young 6 years old who bought papers in bundles of 100. The wholesale rise in cost from 50 cents to 60 cents per bundle increased the personal liability of unsold papers and seriously crippled the already meager newsboy earnings that averaged 26 cents per day. So, beginning July 21, 1899, many New York City newsboys impacted distribution across the northeast by refusing to distribute Joseph Pulitzer's *World*[4] newspaper and William Randolph Hearst's *Journal*.[5] When Pulitzer and Hearst finally agreed to buy back any unsold papers, the two-week strike ended, and the newsboys went back to work.

---

[2] *Newsies*. Directed by Kenny Ortega. Produced by Michael Finnell. Written by Bob Tzudiker and Noni White. Produced by Walt Disney Pictures and distributed by Buena Vista Pictures, 1992.

[3] *Newsies the Musical*. Playwright Harvey Fierstein, Lyricist Jack Feldman, and Composer Alan Menken. Broadway, 2012-14. Won the 2012 Tony Award® for *Best Original Score* and *Best Choreography*, and 2012 *Drama Desk Award for Outstanding Music*.

[4] Published in New York City from 1860 until 1931, and owned by Joseph Pulitzer from 1883 to 1911, and owned by his heirs until the family sold it in 1931.

[5] Originally called the *New York Journal* with morning and evening editions and published from 1895 to 1937.

God instituted an ongoing income to company employees for centuries through the sacrificial system. The people of the Israelite nation gave offerings as a sign of their allegiance to and willingness to obey and honor God, and those gifts in turn were used to support God's special division of workers known as the Levite tribe and priests. The daily, weekly, and special offerings of food, drink, and money were apportioned and passed along as wages.

The Boss also arranged to pay other nations for their labor on His behalf. After Nebuchadnezzar, king of Babylon, fought against the city of Tyre, God told Ezekiel:

"(He) drove his army in a hard campaign against Tyre; every head was rubbed bare and every shoulder made raw," the Lord said. "Yet he and his army got no reward from the campaign he led against Tyre." So, the Boss instructed Ezekiel to announce, "Therefore this is what the Sovereign Lord says: I am going to give Egypt to Nebuchadnezzar king of Babylon, and he will carry off its wealth. He will loot and plunder the land as pay for his army. I have given him Egypt as a reward for his efforts because he and his army did it for me, declares the Sovereign Lord" (Ezekiel 29:17-20).

God additionally provided extra special pay in unique circumstances. For example, after the nation of Midian's betrayal and attempts to corrupt and seduce the Israelite people, God instructed Moses to send a contingent of soldiers to battle against the Midianites. The Israelites selected 1000 soldiers from each tribe (12,000 total) to represent the nation and to go fight for them.

When the soldiers returned with the spoils of war, they brought everything to Moses and Eleazar the priest. At God's direction, the 12,000 soldiers who fought the battle received 50% of the spoils, and the nation received the other 50%. From among the 50% received by the soldiers, the soldiers gave one out of every 500 to Eleazar to honor God. From among the 50% received by the nation, the people gave one out of every 50 to the Levite tribe to honor God.

Though Eleazar and the Levite (and thirteenth tribe) contributed no soldiers to that battle, they served the people and soldiers by doing God's work on behalf of the entire nation full-time. Therefore, the gifts honored God by honoring those who served both God and the people regularly.

Additionally, the commanders of the 1000 soldiers of each tribe, and their sub-commanders over each division of 100 soldiers, all realized that none, not even one single Israelite soldier, fell in the battle. The commanders expressed their sincere gratitude for this unusual blessing by giving all the plundered gold to Moses and Eleazar, who then banked the 420 pounds worth in the tabernacle (Numbers 31).

These stories collectively exemplify several management practices and principles related to providing payment:

- Pay fair wages
- Reward loyalty
- Celebrate success
- Reward abundantly those who do the work
- Share some bounty with everyone involved in any collective team task
- Give thanks to God in ways that benefit others
- Show added gratitude when extra graciously blessed

Grateful, Generous BOSSES

When the Australian family-owned bus company, Grenda Corporation, sold its 66-year old transit operations in 2011, the company founder and his sons decided to reward their 1800-member staff for their contributions to the company's success.

Founder Ken Grenda, along with sons Geoff and Scott, expressed their gratitude by dividing $15 million dollars into bonus amounts based on years of service and position. Employees who had worked for as little as 3 months to as long as 52 years received surprise bonuses in their bank accounts averaging $8,500 and ranging from $1,000 to as much as $30,000.

"A business is only as good as its people, and our people are fantastic," Grenda said. "This is to recognise that. We have grown from just four bus routes in Dandenong in 1945 to operating 1300 buses in Melbourne, Adelaide and Perth. You only get there if you have good people."

According to one employee, "Some employees were calling their banks assuming it was an error. Good bosses are hard to find, and Ken was a very good boss, one of a kind."[6]

Grateful, Generous EMPLOYEES

Seattle, Washington-based entrepreneur, Dan Price, gained notoriety in April 2015 when he announced plans to raise all of Gravity Payments' 120 employee's salaries to a minimum of $70,000, and reduce his own $1.1 million CEO salary to match. His announcement generated more than 500

---

[6] "Meet Victoria's best boss who gave his staff a $15m bonus," Elissa Doherty, 31 January 2012, *The Advertiser*, AdelaideNow.com.au.

million responses on social media and NBC's video of the news story became the most shared video in network history.

Grateful employees responded just over a year later by saving up enough over six months to present Price with his dream car, a Tesla, which had a starting price at the time of, you guessed it, $70,000.[7]

---

[7] "Employees just bought a Tesla for their CEO because he raised minimum salaries to $70,000," Julie Bort, 14 July 2016, BusinessInsider.com.

12
Provide People

I n one of the very first recorded management observations, God acknowledges the need for an associate. After summarizing everything else about creation as "good" and "very good," the first negative God mentions is, "It is not good for the man to be alone. I will make a helper suitable for him" (Genesis 2:18). Thus, Adam and Eve become the first company couple to meet and marry on the job, combine business with pleasure, pursue life/work harmony, enjoy a housing allowance, experience concerns about what to wear to work, and get one another in trouble with their boss.

The trend continued when God provided Noah's wife, three sons, and their wives to serve as his work companions, and again when God provided Moses with a work companion – his brother, Aaron.

> "You shall speak to him and put words in his mouth," God told Moses. "I will help both of you speak and will teach you what to do. He will speak to the people for you and it will be as if he were your mouth and as if you were God to him" (Exodus 4:15-16).

Over time, as the workload increased, Moses eventually reached a point of frustration and exhaustion and scheduled a meeting with his boss to share his feelings and frustrations candidly.

"Why have you brought this trouble on your servant? What have I done to displease you that you put the burden of all these people on me? Did I conceive all these people? Did I give them birth? Why do you tell me to carry them in my arms, as a nurse carries an infant, to the land you promised on oath to their forefathers? I cannot carry all these people by myself; the burden is too heavy for me. If this is how you are going to treat me, put me to death right now – if I have found favor in your eyes – and do not let me face my own ruin" (Numbers 11:10-15).

> *I cannot carry all these people by myself; the burden is too heavy for me. If this is how you are going to treat me, put me to death right now.*

God listened to Moses' complaints, then compassionately replied by instructing Moses to bring 70 of Israel's elders, known leaders and officials, and promised to "take of the Spirit that is on you and put the Spirit on them. They will help you carry the burden of the people so that you will not have to carry it alone" (Numbers 11:16-17).

The good news? Moses gained 70 people to help share the load. The bad news? Moses apparently carried the workload of 71 people prior to asking for help!

People Power

In 1970, David and Barbara Green invested $600 in a home-based business making miniature picture frames. They opened their first 300-square-foot Hobby Lobby store in Oklahoma City two years later, eventually growing to more than 750 stores and the largest privately-owned arts-and-crafts retailer in the world with approximately 32,000 employees and operating in forty-seven states. [1]

In 1905, Florence Butt invested $60 in opening the C.C. Butt Grocery Store in Kerrville, Texas. Today H-E-B serves families all over Texas and Mexico in 155 communities, with more than 340 stores and over 100,000 employees. [2]

In 1992, Gary and Diane Heavin opened their first Curves women's fitness club in 1992 in Harlingen, Texas. After opening a second successful club they believed they had tapped into something that could help millions of women, but they knew they needed help. They needed passionate people interested in helping women in their communities and who would be interested in learning how to run a Curves. They opened their first franchise in Paris, Texas in 1995. By their 25th anniversary on September 17, 2017, they had become one of the largest chains of fitness clubs for women in the world with more than 4,000 locations in over 70 countries. [3]

In 1970, Tom and Kate Chappell borrowed $5,000 to create a business rooted in their passion to use natural, unprocessed foods and unadulterated products that would not harm the environment. Now a division of multinational

---

[1] "Our Story," HobbyLobby.com.
[2] "About," HEB.com.
[3] "About us," Curves.com.

conglomerate Colgate-Palmolive, Tom's of Maine has about 150 employees, and its 90 or so oral- and body-care products are sold at more than 40,000 retail outlets worldwide.[4]

In 1950, John Searcy began selling automotive batteries out of the trunk of his Studebaker pickup. He founded Interstate Battery System in 1952, which has grown into billion dollar privately held corporation powered by a Distributor network of 300 wholesale warehouses with more than 200,000 dealers around the world and 200 All Battery Center franchise stores.[5]

In 1948, Harry and Esther Snyder introduced California's first drive-thru hamburger stand in 10-foot square spot at Francisquito and Garvey in Baldwin Park. Harry visited the markets every morning to pick out fresh ingredients to prepare by hand, while Esther handled all the accounting at home. Since then, the privately owned In-N-Out Burger has grown to nearly 350 locations in more than 6 states.[6]

On Friday, September 13, 1963, Mary Kay Ash opened Beauty by Mary Kay in a 500-square-foot storefront in Dallas, Texas funded by her $5,000 life savings. By 2015, the company employed approximately 5000 staff supporting 3.5 million Mary Kay Independent Beauty Consultants around the world with revenues in excess of $3.7 billion.[7]

Many organizations begin with a vision and take shape through the work of entrepreneurial, passionate founders. Some eventually experience seasons of explosive growth and attain great net worth, while others grow more in health and

---

[4] "Our Company," TomsOfMaine.com.

[5] "History," InterstateBatteries.com.

[6] "History," In-N-Out.com.

[7] "Quick Facts," MayKay.com, and "DSN Global 100: The Top Direct Selling Companies in the World," Direct Selling News, 31 May 2016.

longevity than in size or wealth. Commonalities include the exponential power of people who share the vision and have opportunities to share the workload. Teamwork is team work, and bossing often involves assembling and managing the team – providing people – needed for organizational growth and health. Lack of quality, key people can translate to loss and decline, and ultimately sabotage mission and vision.

An administrator constantly felt overwhelmed and overworked. He pondered various possibilities – his own inefficiency, insufficient training, or possibly unrealistic expectations from his boss and co-workers. However, not knowing, and rather than take his situation personally or leave in frustration, he decided to review other similar companies in attempt to gain an unbiased perspective.

> *Commonalities include the exponential power of people who share the vision and have opportunities to share the workload.*

Utilizing a graph that correlated the number of clients (engaged constituents) versus the number of personnel (staff size) performing comparable duties in other organizations, the administrator discovered that the staffing of other similar companies closely fit a standard trend line. According to the observed standard, the administrator's company should have employed a department of 9 people doing what 2.5 employees were attempting to accomplish in his department in his organization.

His boss initially laughed at his research and rejected his proposed hiring plan that included detailed job descriptions, a budget, a timeline for adding 6.5 new employees to meet the organization's needs adequately, and an interim plan to reign in unrealistic employee expectations and match other healthy organizational standards.

Thankfully, his thorough research did help set in motion a positive sequence of events. Rationalizing the problems with outside information helped the employee understand that crazy, lazy, or stupid were not appropriately self-defining characteristics. Leadership and staff in their own and other departments gained new perspectives on their overall situations, including purpose, roles, structure, and healthy workload. And, they eventually gained approval to begin adding and restructuring staff according to the well-defined, long-range plan.

Providing employees with people they need to help do their job(s) or do them even better can happen in numerous ways – reassigning current employees, assembling a team of current employees, hiring new employees, contracting with outside associates or vital vendors, and/or incorporating volunteers. Though tempting to give busy people more work because they tend to get more work done, or to think of ourselves as heroes because we can do it all if we just overwork more, bossing like God includes helping others and ourselves find and maintain a healthy life and workload harmony – including finding more people to help.

Also, just because someone CAN do something, and even do it very well, does not mean they SHOULD do that thing at certain times. Some people can do many things very well, but there is often no healthy way to do them all well at the same time. In view of Ecclesiastes 3:1, "There is a time for everything, and a season for every activity under the heavens," there may be appropriate times to pick some things up and lay others down, even if only for a season.

Although some managers gain well-deserved reputations for mostly doing nothing, others try to do too much. Rather than oversee all that needs to be done and work with others to do it, they try to do it all. Bossing like God means making sure ALL of one's people have ALL the people they need to do their job(s), and ALL includes bosses.

Employees can help conduct thorough research, offer well-thought out plans and proposals to address identified needs, serve diligently and wholeheartedly, and seek additional help when needed. In a truly selfless move, some employees may even recommend others more suited to their current role to replace them, and thankful bosses can reward them by helping them advance to more befitting positions.

Just because we can do something, and even do it very well, that does not mean we should.

Providing people often involves a dynamic game of mixing and matching, adding and subtracting, all relative to the needs of each situation at the time. In this arena, bossing significantly relates to people, not tasks, especially people's need for other people to share the journey as well as the load.

13
Provide Perspective

The ability to provide perspective is one reason some people lead. Their experiences, insights, intelligence, and knack often help them see the big picture, think beyond the visible horizon, and make far-reaching decisions and plans in such a way that bossing is their best fit in an organization. Bosses also typically have access to more information, act according to broader purposes, and have deeper understandings of the ramifications of even the smallest of actions, possibilities, and trends.

When God called Abram to leave his homeland and move to a new land to father a new nation, God granted the childless man a new vision of a distant and glorious future worth the cost of relocating. By reframing 100-year old Abram as "*Abraham*" (father of many nations) and 90-year old barren Sarai as "*Sarah*" (mother of nations), the Boss provided them with reformatted perspectives of themselves (Genesis 17).

When *Elijah* ran in fear for his life from the evil Queen Jezebel, he complained to God, "I have been very zealous for the Lord God Almighty. The Israelites have rejected your covenant, torn down your altars, and put your prophets to death with the sword. I am the only one left, and now they are trying to kill me too" (I Kings 19). However, God informed Elijah of 7,000 others in the nation kept on "reserve" and not corrupt. This revelation gave Elijah a new perspective of himself as a member of a large team on a field rather than a solo act alone on stage.

Elijah's successor helped provide a similarly revealing perspective to his employee. After a nearby king set out to kill *Elisha* and surrounded their city one night with his army, Elisha's servant cried out in distress and in fear for their lives. However, Elisha informed him that they were not alone and asked his Boss to open the servant's eyes "so he may see." The servant's glimpse into the spiritual realm revealed that they were under the protection of God's vast army – "he looked and saw the hills full of horses and chariots of fire all around Elisha" (II Kings 6:8-23).

> *By reframing...the Boss provided them with reformatted perspectives.*

When *Job* complained about his circumstances and questioned God, God responded with such a grand inquisition that Job gained a new perspective of himself, "Surely I spoke of things I did not understand...My ears had heard of you but now my eyes have seen you. Therefore I despise myself and repent in dust and ashes" (Job 42:3,6). Job also gained a new perspective on God as brilliant Creator and Lord Almighty over everyone and everything (1 - 42).

When *Jonah* bitterly complained about his personal circumstances, God provided a perspective different from the lowly, self-centered one the reluctant prophet voiced. After finally going to Nineveh to warn the city of their impending destruction unless they repented, Jonah awaited their deaths.

However, when the citizens listened and repented – and God responded to their humility with grace – Jonah got angry. In his anger, he stalked over to sit on a hill in the heat of the day to watch and wait for God to destroy them anyway. God initially had compassion on him and provided a plant to shade his sulky servant from the sun, but then Jonah got mad at God for killing the plant God grew over him to protect him.

When Jonah whined, "It would be better for me to die than to live," God replied, "Is it right for you to be angry about the plant?" To which Jonah replied, "It is. And I'm so angry I wish I were dead," and to which God responded, "You have been concerned about this plant, though you did not tend it or make it grow. It sprang up overnight and died overnight. And should I not have concern for the great city of Nineveh, in which there are more than a hundred and twenty thousand people who cannot tell their right hand from their left, and many cattle as well?" (Jonah 4)

God sought to provide Jonah a higher perspective by contrasting his feelings of frustration with the real lives of tens of thousands of people and animals. While many might have rejoiced that their message prevailed and helped save lives, Jonah focused on himself and squelched his potential for joy via his preference for self-satisfaction.

Providing perspective can include the following:

- *Reminding* people why they do what they do
- *Reframing* thinking
- *Refocusing* efforts
- *Refining* self-image
- *Recasting* vision and plans for the long game

Sometimes people need reminding that their jobs are not just all about them; that their circumstances may pale in comparison to those of others on occasion; that there are bigger, higher purposes; that their actions can affect history beyond them; that gratitude is preferable to complaint; and that they are *not* the boss. And, some bosses need reminding that *they* are not the Supreme Boss of all bosses.

Reframing the Universe

Once upon a time, in a galaxy not very far away, some Industrial Light and Magic (ILM) employees and others working with George Lucas on the first Stars Wars film really had no idea what their director was talking about. Specifically, they did not understand lightsabers, Jedi Knights, jawas, droids, holographics, R2-D2, the Force, and the Death Star.

These were not only new concepts. The technology needed to bring Lucas's vision of the Star Wars universe to the movie screen did not exist at the time. Therefore, he assembled a team to invent a new generation of special effects while also launching a company that changed the course of the movie business, as well as media entertainment through derivatives such as Pixar and Photoshop.

According to Industrial Light and Magic's own retelling of their historical and adventurous beginnings, the company "was born in a sweltering warehouse behind the Van Nuys airport in the summer of 1975. Its first employees were recent college graduates (and dropouts) with rich imaginations and nimble fingers. They were tasked with building Star Wars' creatures, spaceships, circuit boards, and cameras. It didn't go smoothly or even on schedule, but the skilled work of ILM's fledgling artists, technicians, and engineers transported audiences into galaxies far, far away."[1]

> *Their boss's perspective had to suffice for their own understanding until they could see the big picture for themselves.*

Lucas' agent and lawyer did not really understand the story either, even while they were pitching it to the eventual buyer, Twentieth Century Fox. In fact, Fox President Alan Ladd Jr. worked with Lucas for over four years and only saw the film for the first time the week before release. He recalled his efforts to get studio approval to make the epic space opera.[2]

"How do you do a synopsis of this movie for a board of directors? Imagine saying, 'There is a Wookie named Chewbacca and...' All I can say is that the man got a performance out of a robot."[3]

The movie's creators performed their work under the direction of Lucas. They collaborated to sell something they did not really understand, to create special effects in ways never done before, and to bring something to the big screen that some of them did not understand until they saw the first film. Only then did many members of their team realize the larger perspective and contributions of their work. Along the way, their boss's perspective had to suffice for their own understanding until they could see the big picture for themselves.

---

[1] "The Untold Story of ILM, a Titan That Forever Changed Film," Alex French and Howie Kahn, May 2015, WIRED magazine, WIRED.com.

[2] "A television or radio drama or motion picture that is a science-fiction adventure story," Dictionary.com.

[3] "Lucas: Film-Maker With the Force," Paul Rosenfield, 5 June 1977, LATimes.com.

14
Provide Place

A fair amount of scripture describes God's work to provide appropriate places and spaces for His employees to live and work and play. Certainly, of all of whom it has been said, "They built their business from nothing," God seems literally the only one who really did. Moreover, providing a place appears among the first acts recorded in the biblical text.

Amidst the campus of the universe, the Boss placed *Adam and Eve* in a living and working paradise, the Garden of Eden. In the beginning, they did not have to worry about commuting, where to park, what to wear to work, where to eat, where to have a meeting, who had the best office view, or vacations or overtime or much of anything. Their places and spaces were elegant, and infinitely more than adequate.

God gave *Noah* the opportunity to build his own office, as well as a benefits package that included a yearlong family cruise, membership to the zoo, and relocation assistance.

From the first moment *Abraham* appears until the time of Solomon (numerous centuries), God works to provide dedicated, vibrant, healthy places for those He employs.

- Abraham's move initiated the establishment of a home place in the general area known as the *LAND of Israel.*

- Joseph's transition from slave to master in Egypt provided God's infant people a place to incubate and grow into the *PEOPLE of Israel.*

- Moses' leadership helped make way for the Promised Land and people to converge and become the *NATION of Israel.* "I am sending an angel ahead of you," the Lord told Moses, "to guard you along the way and to bring you to the place I have prepared" (Exodus 23:20).

The ensuing leadership of Joshua, various judges, the prophet Samuel, and kings Saul and David and Solomon, all were part of God's plan to provide His treasured possession, His nation, a place to call their own – the Promised Land (Israel). "I will provide a place for my people Israel," God said, "and will plant them so that they can have a home of their own and no longer be disturbed" (II Samuel 7:10).

However, after settling into their long-promised land, the people continued to rebel. "So the Lord was very angry with Israel and removed them from his presence...he afflicted them and gave them into the hands of plunderers until he thrust them from his presence" (II Kings 17:7-20).

Thereafter, God's promises offered repeatedly through the prophets included a recurring promise to prepare a new place for His people. Whether the references were to a *reunited kingdom,* a *revitalized Jerusalem,* a *return from exile,* or *resurrection to new life* in a new heavens and new earth, the idea of God providing a place for His people recurs throughout most of the prophetic books.

Their Boss promises, "You will live in the land I gave your forefathers; you will be my people, and I will be your God" and "My dwelling place will be with them; I will be their God, and they will be my people" (Ezekiel 36:28, 37:27).

From Genesis through Revelation, God aims to provide a place for His people, as revealed in promises and expectations that weave thematically throughout Scripture.

Engineering Place and Space

(KLL) My engineering background probably explains why an intentional focus on elements related to place and space seems normal and practical. My planning often includes efforts to perceive things as others might experience them.

As a pastor, I visited my congregations in their homes and workplaces, sat in various locations among sanctuary pews, meandered into offices and classrooms, walked through all the doors of my churches and drove by as if a stranger to ponder the view from those perspectives.

As a business executive, my work has included visiting clients on-location near and far to attempt to understand who they are and what they do, and to help them gain outside perspectives on how others experience what they offer, where and how they offer it, and offer suggestions for improvement.

As an educational administrator, I visit the offices of employees, classrooms of students, and campuses of hosts to try to gain a sense of our work, learning, and study spaces.

In my work with both profit and non-profit organizations, I like to step back, drive into our parking lots, walk into our offices and around our campuses, and review our materials and services while pretending I am a visitor, a member, a potential employee, a donor, and even a competitor.

Our journeys toward providing appropriate, inviting, effective, efficient, and productive places have included everything from simple cleanups and repairs all the way to buying new furnishings, new land, and building new facilities. We've expanded, downsized, improved lighting and sound, redecorated, reorganized, repainted, resupplied, and moved.

In some cases, rescheduling the timing of indoor cleaning or outdoor mowing and blowing has helped provide vastly improved learning environments. In others, we solved style issues by switching the office locations of employees, solved taste issues by offering new menus, solved time issues by altering schedules, and solved irritating traffic issues by designing and implementing new patterns and timings of traffic flow.

> *Bossing like God involves working to provide healthy, productive places for mission engagement.*

Interestingly, I also have experience working toward NOT providing spaces that our organization can uniquely call our own. In one of our educational models, we collaborate with others who *do* have available places to provide short-term, dedicated educational space. The result has been that we view the world as our campus, and host locations in regional proximity communities as our classrooms. Thus, we have a variety of team members in numerous locations who all work together to provide a network of places that provide rich and diverse experiences for our students and faculty. Ironically, we spend a great deal of time coordinating these spaces, but bossing like God means that we should be doing exactly that very thing – working to provide healthy, productive places for mission engagement.

Reflection

(BDM) The consequences of not enabling conducive circumstances for employees' need for place can devastate a team's effectiveness and negatively affect their journey.

I once failed to uphold my part of a job in this regard. I had an employee responsible for serving a customer and whose task revolved around making himself available and locally present so he could actively listen to the needs of our customer. Building genuine relationships, understanding problems, and collaborating to develop innovative solutions in conjunction with our talented teams and technologies required close proximity to the customer. The job required a physical location on-site within their primary research and development workspace. Unfortunately for us, their work area required top-level security clearance and heightened safety training due to the volatile materials that were part of their experimentations and product development.

No one in our organization had ever previously received such clearance with this customer. Nevertheless, with access critical to our purpose and vision, I pursued unconventional methods to work to equip my employee with the locale and resources necessary for success.

However, the process took a year to obtain the necessary clearance. During that time, we did not achieve any of our key performance objectives, resulting in a variety of negative consequences along the way. Thankfully, resolution of the PLACE issue proved extremely beneficial and we eventually achieved success. The experience helped me realize that providing a place can sometimes make or break performance results, and bosses bear primary responsibility.

15

Provide Presence

Although some might question this, God's actions reveal a priority commitment to personal presence in various forms, at various appropriate times, and as warranted.

During Adam and Eve's sojourn in the Garden of Eden, God apparently shared a presence with them described in the text as the Lord God "walking in the garden in the cool of the day" (Genesis 3:8). This was probably awesome up until they disobeyed God and violated the single prohibition in their contract. Then, like some employees today, they scrambled when they heard the Boss walking in their direction. Part of their punishment included expulsion from this unique presence with their Boss in the Garden of Eden.

Then, after Adam and Eve's first son, Cain, killed his brother, Abel, God instituted consequences. Cain then decried, "My punishment is more than I can bear. Today you are driving me from the land, and I will be hidden from your presence...So Cain went out from the Lord's presence and lived in the land of Nod east of Eden" (Genesis 4:14, 16). Cain mourned the loss of the same presence of God that believers desire and seek, and that skeptics deny even exists.

Giant Contrasts

When prominent Evangelist Billy Graham and renowned Physicist Stephen Hawking died within weeks of each other in early 2018, their contrasting beliefs about God and heaven could not have been any more opposite.

Though married for 30 years to his first wife, Jane Beryl Wilde Hawking Jones,[1] a devout Christian, Stephen Hawking believed "There is no god. No one created our universe, and no one directs our fate. This leads me to a profound realization; There is probably no heaven, and no afterlife either. We have this one life to appreciate the grand design of the universe, and for that I am extremely grateful."[2]

In a 2004 article in *The Atlantic* magazine that referenced the Hawkings' marital struggles, author Tim Adams noted, "Jane took much of her dramatic hope at the time from her faith, and still sees something of the irony in the fact that her Christianity gave her the strength to support her husband, the most profound atheist. 'Stephen, I hope, had belief in me that I could make everything possible for him, but he did not share my religious – or spiritual – faith.'"[3]

Hawking summarized his expectation following death this way, "I regard the brain as a computer which will stop working when its components fail. There is no heaven or afterlife for broken down computers; that is a fairy story for people afraid of the dark."[4]

---

[1] Hawking and Wilde married in 1965 and divorced in 1995. She married Jonathan Jones in 1997.

[2] Hawking in 2011 while narrating the first episode of the American television series "Curiosity," Directed by Darlow Smithson, Discovery-Gaiam, 2012.

[3] "Jane Hawking: Brief history of a first wife," Tim Adams, 3 April 2004, *The Atlantic*.

[4] Ian Sample, "Stephen Hawking: 'There Is No Heaven; It's a Fairy Story'," 15 May 2011, *The Guardian*.

On the other hand, Graham famously stated, as widely reported following his death, "Someday you will read or hear that Billy Graham is dead. Don't you believe a word of it. I shall be more alive than I am now. I will just have changed my address. I will have gone into the presence of God."[5]

In a tribute to his wife of 64 years, Ruth Bell Graham, who died over ten years earlier in 2007, Billy commented, "In her last days she talked repeatedly of heaven, and although I will miss her more than I can possibly say, I rejoice that someday soon we will be reunited in the presence of the Lord she loved and served so faithfully."[6]

Meanwhile, Back in the Desert

After God called Moses into His employ, Moses at one point reminded God that He had been telling him to lead the people, "But you have not let me know whom you will send with me." When God replied, "My Presence will go with you," Moses exclaimed, "If your Presence does not go with us, do not send us up from here. How will anyone know that you are pleased with me and with your people unless you go with us? What else will distinguish me and your people from all the other people on the face of the earth?" (Exodus 33:12-16).

This distinguishing Presence mentioned here by Moses is regularly depicted in the biblical text as distinctly unique. God's Presence also variously manifests in different forms.

Consider God's appearance as a man to Abraham (Genesis 18), as a wrestler with Jacob (Genesis 32:22-30), as Supreme Commander to Joshua (Joshua 5:15-6:5), as Commissioner to

---

[5] "Billy Graham: God's Ambassador," Photo biography published by the Billy Graham Evangelistic Association, 1999.

[6] "Billy Graham dies: His tribute to his wife, Ruth," 21 Feb 2018, Citizen-Times.com.

Gideon (Judges 6), and as an unquenchable figure described as a "son of the gods" walking around in the fiery furnace with Shadrach, Meshach, and Abednego (Daniel 3:25).

Moses first met God on remote location at His burning bush office (Exodus 3). His itinerant Presence then traveled with the Israelites in a pillar of cloud by day and a pillar of fire by night where everyone, night or day, could look up and see the physical evidence of God's Presence in the camp for nearly 40 years! He met with Moses for an extended retreat at one of His summit offices on Mount Sinai, as well as in temporary central offices in the tent of meeting and the Tabernacle.

God appeared in splendor to Moses, Aaron, Nadab and Abihu, and seventy of the elders of Israel at a specially called conference meeting and banquet (Exodus 24).

He appeared in dreams and visions to Jacob at the top of a ladder (Genesis 28:10-22), to Solomon (I Kings 3 and 9), to Isaiah (Isaiah 6), Jeremiah (Jeremiah 1), Ezekiel, Daniel, and others as recorded in various books in the Bible.

The Boss manifested His Presence over the Ark of the Covenant (Exodus 25:10-22), in association with the Book of the Law (Deuteronomy 31), in chariots and horses of fire (II Kings 2:11 and 6:17), in plagues (Exodus 7-12), and in the sound of marching in the trees (II Samuel 5:24), as well as through numerous and varied people filled with His Spirit.

God's Presence in these situations appeared as gloriously and powerfully unique, distinct from all else around Him, and often resulted in significant life changes, proved instructive, cautionary, pleasing in some cases and frightening in others, awe-inspiring, and more.

Of course, this is exactly the same effect most bosses want to have on their employees.

The CEO

Most employees do long for a good relationship with their boss, to enjoy their presence, to be inspired by them, coached and trained by them, awed by them, and even respectfully fearful of them. Unfortunately, some are not so blessed and experience greater pleasure when their bosses are absent. Therefore, if you discover that people are happiest when you as their boss are gone, perhaps something is awry.

> ***The Goldilocks Challenge*** *requires bosses to provide presence that is neither too hot nor too cold.*

One CEO under scrutiny as part of a company-wide evaluation sadly discovered that most of his employees thought he was mean. He did not think of himself as mean and was genuinely disappointed in himself. Yet, rather than respond with blame or subversion, he took responsibility for his behavior.

"I decided to change," he says, "so I did. I had to learn how to communicate differently, how to have real relationships, and how to be equally and even more effective in other ways."

A boss's presence is not necessarily related to control, or intrusion, or continually monitoring employees who might want to play more and work less. Rather, a balanced presence is about nurturing a healthy, productive relationship that fosters an environment where employers and employees enjoy working together as a team.

The Goldilocks Challenge

Providing presence does not mean that bosses should always be physically present in an employee's workspace either. Ecclesiastes 7:18 cautions balance by encouraging the avoidance of extremes. Relative to proximity, "The Goldilocks Challenge" requires bosses to provide presence that is neither too hot nor too cold, too little nor too much, too involved nor not involved enough, and neither too present nor too absent.

The Desk Test

Some employees walk by a boss's office, or vice versa, and think that if someone is not sitting at their desk, then that person must not be working. In the observer's mind, a person is absent from their paradigm appearance of "working."

"It must be nice," they might say or think sarcastically, "to dip in to work occasionally, and leave the rest of us to slave it out 8 hours a day."

"The Desk Test" can certainly be revelatory and relevant in some industries, such as a stationary post where an absent worker in an assembly line results in incomplete assembly. However, in other work situations, NOT sitting in an office at a desk may be when work IS getting done because working outside of the office is a key element of the job.

Some people work outside of 8 a.m. to 5 p.m. boundaries. Some attend early morning or evening events and meetings, or work extremely long sequences of consecutive hours on consecutive days, and they must find their balance in working less during what are often seen as "normal working hours."

A perceived absent boss, or employee, may sometimes actually work more than everyone else because much of their work is performed out of sight of those who think they are not working. In these circumstances, it can be helpful to provide follow up reporting on results. Additionally, highlighting helpful insights and productive outcomes resulting from boondoggles can help provide vital contextual insights and appreciation for potential next steps that might involve other people on a team, as well as shared opportunities to think through challenges and share the joys of fruitful engagements.

Some people blame God for not passing "The Desk Test" at times. Some think He only worked six days total and has been resting up top in the heavenly penthouse or rocking on His front porch ever since. Other people, like Stephen Hawking, doubt a Big Boss in a heavenly Executive Office even exists at all. Conversely, like Hawking's first wife and the Grahams, many believe God is still present on the job, working both directly Himself, as well as indirectly through His employees.

> *Some bosses need to physically show up and interrelate more so that their people realize that they do exist and are working, while others need to back off and give their employees less presence.*

Ultimately, a healthy balance means intentionally striving to provide appropriate presence. Some bosses need to physically show up and interrelate more so that their people realize that they do exist and are working, while others need to back off and reduce their overbearing presence.

16
Provide Primer

After hiking all day in the New Mexico mountains, a group arrived at their remote campsite tired, hungry, and very thirsty. The map of that location indicated a well, clearly identified upon arrival by the red-handled hand pump standing alone in the middle of a clearing. However, pumping the handle failed to deliver any refreshment from the ground below. Alas, the long-awaited for well seemed dry. Or was it?

"I think pumps nccd to be primed to work," someone said.

"How do we do that?"

"If we pour some water in the top, then work the handle, that should get the water flowing."

The idea of pouring what precious little water anyone had left into an apparently dry well seemed ridiculous, and no one offered any of theirs to try it.

Finally, one brave soul ventured forth, selflessly emptied what remained in his canteen into the top, and then began pumping. After a few empty pumps, the handle indicated an increase in pressure, a sound began to gurgle below, and then beautiful streams of water burst forth with each pump, much to the delight and relief of everyone.

Basic Survival

God purposefully founded a new nation through which He planned to bless the whole earth through Abraham, his son Isaac, and grandson Jacob. While reviewing the business plans for their descendants with Moses, God explained, "If you obey me fully and keep my covenant, then out of all nations you will be my treasured possession. Although the whole earth is mine, you will be for me a kingdom of priests and a holy nation" (Exodus 19:5-6).

But the Hebrew's wilderness adventures between their exodus from Egypt and arrival in the Promised Land involved daunting years of desert travel where provisions proved scarce. Many times people were tired, hungry, and very thirsty. So, God primed the pump of the fledgling "holy nation" to help get things flowing.

Strange "bread from Heaven," which the people called "manna,"[1] first appeared in the wilderness after their exodus and ended the day after they ate their first meal sourced in the Promised Land (Exodus 16 through Joshua 5:10-12). This provision occurred 6 days a week, with double the amount on the sixth day so they could rest on the seventh day, every week, every month, and every year for a total of nearly 40 years! When Jesus later taught his disciples to pray and included the phrase, "Give us this day our daily bread" (Matthew 6:11), his disciples understood this contextual reference to God's provision of daily bread to their ancestors.

Special provisions of quail appeared on the wilderness menu at least twice (Exodus 16 and Numbers 11), and both the gifts of manna and quail required labor contributions from the people in order to partake of the provisions.

---

[1] The word "manna" means "What is it?"

God also provided water. There were springs in desert, but some locations had no adequate water supply, and yet great need. In one case, God told Moses to strike a rock in order to prime the pump (Exodus 17), and in another case, God directed Moses to simply speak to the designated rock (Numbers 20).[2]

During this season, God directly provided the basic needs of the nation. He also had a long-term plan to meet their basic needs once they entered the Promised Land. In doing so, God primed His people for survival and success by giving them what they needed to live, grow, and serve faithfully.

> *God primed His people for survival and success by giving them what they need to live, grow, and serve faithfully.*

Sometimes bossing like God includes providing primer to help people survive, helping things get started, and beginning a long-term plan and practices to help meet basic needs.

Training, Tools, and Equipment

When God hired Moses, Moses initially balked at the job offer because he did not think he had the right stuff for the field of endeavor offered. Nor did he believe he had the right tools and equipment to do the job.

However, God immediately responded to Moses's doubts by asking, "What is that in your hand?"

"A staff," Moses replied.

---

[2] In the latter case, Moses disobeyed God's instructions. He struck the rock twice and spoke angrily to the people at the very time God planned to uplift him in front of the nation and show them that Moses was so powerful he could just speak to a rock to bring forth water. However, because he dishonored and disobeyed his boss in public, Moses did not get to enter the Promised Land, even after 40 years of mostly great leadership.

God then proceeded to show Moses how to use the one tool he already had, not only on hand, but literally in his hand. When Moses continued to balk, claiming lack of eloquence and slowness of speech and tongue, God exasperatingly pointed out that He made Moses' mouth and would help him speak and teach him what to say (Exodus 4).

Centuries later – after Moses and Joshua and ensuing generations combined to complete Moses' original mission of leading the people out of Egypt and firmly establishing them in their own land – Solomon began building the temple in Jerusalem. God primed him with training, tools, and equipment provided through his father, David, and the assistance of other key leaders (see I Kings 6:1 and I Chronicles 28-29).

> *Sometimes when a well seems dry, all that is needed is a hand pump and a brave, selfless soul with a little water.*

Occasionally, people have what they need to do what needs to be done, but they do not know how to get started. Other times, people know what to do, but lack what they need to do their job well. Bossing like God in these cases may involve providing primer in the form of training, tools, or equipment. After all, sometimes when a well seems dry, all that is needed is a hand pump and a brave, selfless soul with a little water.

What Is That In Your Hand?

When All Saints Episcopal Church in Smyrna, Tennessee welcomed former businessman turned pastor Rev. Michael Spurlock to his first assignment in 2008, the church teetered precariously on the verge of closing. The 20 or so remaining congregants after a church split were unable to pay bills or the mortgage on the facilities and 22-acres of former farmland bordering Stewart Creek, so Spurlock's superiors charged him with closing the church and selling the property.

About the same time, 70 Karen refugees from Myanmar, who had fled to camps in Thailand and eventually resettled in Tennessee, began attending All Saints. The refugees – former farmers and fellow Christians in the worldwide Episcopal Church – needed help with food, clothing, housing, furniture, finding jobs, and transportation. However, they overwhelmed the few church members and meager resources.

Ye Win, a local Karen leader and son of an Anglican missionary, attended All Saints with his wife and trusted God wholeheartedly despite the trauma inflicted on his people since the civil wars began in 1949.[3]

"We are the people of God," Win noted, "even if we are lost, away from our home, even if we are isolated, we are still close to God. God never left our people."[4]

The Wins originally settled in the United States with help from members of a church in New Bern, North Carolina. Helen Dawley, a retired teacher in her 70's and transplant from Florida, found out about the Win's and another couple and reached out to help, and invited others to join her.

---

[3] Since Myanmar (formerly Burma) gained independence from British colonial rule in 1948, the nation has spiraled downward from one of the best educated East Asian countries to one of the least and poorest. Hostilities between the ethnic Bamar Buddhist majority and numerous non-Buddhist ethnic minorities have resulted in more than six decades of ongoing civil war.

[4] "How a group of refugees saved a church on the brink of collapsing," Bob Smietana, 18 August 2017, WashingtonPost.com.

"I had time and a car," Dawley recalls, noting the refugees were here, needed help and she could provide assistance.[5]

Win lived out his gratitude for members of the Rhems congregation by paying it forward to others.

"When I was in the United Methodist church in North Carolina, the families of the congregation helped me. When I got to Tennessee, I helped other families. I believe that was God's plan."[6]

The enterprising leader noticed the All Saint church's unused land and asked Spurlock for permission to plant gardens on the property to help feed the Karen families, and perhaps help the church. Spurlock initially feared the property might be sold before any crop could be harvested.

However, as he and church members considered the idea, they wondered if perhaps God had given them both the land and new congregants for a purpose. Spurlock recalls thinking, "It's God saying, 'I've given you this land, and now I've sent you all these farmers. And they need to eat, and the church needs to provide a means by which they can do that.'"[7]

Church member, Mark Orr recalls, "I'm ashamed to say it, but we had to wait until God slapped us on the head, and said, 'I gave this land to you, put it to work.'"[8]

Bruce Gentry, a local dairy farmer who had once farmed the property, volunteered to plow, and another local farmer gave the church a mobile irrigation tank. Together, the

[5] "Refugees revitalize country church," Heather Hahn, 25 August 2017, United Methodist News Service (UMNS), UMC.org.

[6] "Karen refugees revitalize two mainline churches, inspire film *All Saints*," Amy Sowder and Heather Hahn, 5 September 2017, TheChristianCentury.org.

[7] "Burmese Refugees Provide Small-Town Church with Renewed Purpose," 2 November 2009, VOANews.com

[8] Myanmar refugees reinvigorate Tenn. church," Bob Smietana, 2 December 2008, *The (Nashville) Tennessean*.

refugees, church members, and community volunteers helped plant 16 acres. Ten percent of the successful summer harvest of 20,000 pounds of produce helped feed the Karen refugees, while the rest either went to market or local food pantries. Along with help from the local diocese, the farm's proceeds eventually helped pay off the mortgage and fund other outreach projects.

Providing primer may involve helping people survive, helping things get started with what people have in hand, and launching a long-term plan and practices to help meet basic needs.

The inspirational story of how God used the land and refugees to help the church, and the church to help the refugees and community is told in the movie, *All Saints* (2017), starring John Corbett.[9]

"It's a classic example of the Advent story," volunteer manager of the farm at the time, Michael Williams said. "We could not find God, but God found us. In this case, he appeared to us in the form of 70 people who came from Myanmar."[10]

Reflection

- What do I have in my hand?
- What do my employees have available?
- What do they need?

---

[9] *All Saints*, Directed by Steve Gomer, Affirm Films and Columbia Pictures, 2017.
[10] Myanmar refugees reinvigorate Tenn. church," Bob Smietana, 2 December 2008, *The (Nashville) Tennessean.*

17
Provide Protection

Some of the most disappointing employment experiences occur when bosses fail to protect their employees. Although, as noted earlier, free will complicates things, God does model bosses providing protection.

Adam and Eve

In the beginning, God gave Adam and Eve instructions, and warned about a single danger to protect them from harm.

> "You must not eat fruit from the tree of the knowledge of good and evil, for when you eat of it, you will surely die" (Genesis 2:17).

When they failed to heed the warning, He banished them from the Garden of Eden and placed cherubim and a flaming sword flashing back and forth to guard the way to the tree of life (Genesis 3:24). This protection, strange as it may seem, kept people from living forever in a corrupted state. He also protected their naked bodies by providing clothes (3:21), since life outside the Garden promised less than idyllic prospects.

Cain

Before Cain killed his brother, God warned him about his dangerous attitude (4:6-7). Even after Cain killed Abel and God sent him away from his land and the Lord's presence, God put a mark of protection on Cain so that "no one who found him would kill him" (4:15).

Noah

God notified Noah of impending disaster and instructed him to build the ark as a means of protecting him and his family and select animals preserved to repopulate the earth.

Joseph

God protected Joseph and his entire family from starvation and prepared a place for His people to grow through strange twists and turns in a journey from slave to second-in-command of Egypt.

Israelites

God protected the Israelites from the most devastating plagues brought upon the Egyptians. The plagues of blood, frogs, gnats, and flies affected everyone, but the next six plagues of the death of livestock, boils, hail, locusts, darkness, and death of the firstborn sons and cattle only affected the Egyptians. He opened a dry passage through midst of the Red Sea, placed His pillar of cloud and fire between the Israelites and Egyptians to protect His people (Exodus 14), and protected them throughout their wilderness journeys in many ways. He even offered a wardrobe protection plan that kept everyone's clothes and shoes from wearing out during their nearly 40-year odyssey (Deuteronomy 29:5).

Others

God protected:

- David throughout various run-ins with Saul, various other enemies, and numerous battles.
- Elisha and his servant with chariots and horses of fire (II Kings 6:8-23).
- Hananiah, Mishael, and Azariah – also known by their Babylonian names: Shadrach, Meshach, and Abednego – in the fiery furnace (Daniel 3).
- Daniel in the lion's den (Daniel 6).
- His people in general and some leaders in particular by repeatedly sending prophets (Nehemiah 9:29-31).

Similarly, employers have a responsibility to look out for, backup, defend, safeguard, shield, and warn their employees.

Flip Flopper

Carrie met with her boss to discuss a known and recurring problem in her division. Together, they came up with a plan and the boss assured her that during the annual meeting, he would back her up 100% to take care of the issue.

However, when Carrie addressed the situation during the meeting, her boss not only did not back her up, he publicly ridiculed her for bringing it up. Although the problem existed long before her arrival and had nothing to do with Carrie, her boss exacerbated the issue and undercut her leadership authority. As a result, she no longer trusted her leader, the problem became even more entrenched, and the incident generated a sense of betrayal on one side and entitlement on the other that further divided the groups represented.

Ultimately, by luring Carrie into an action that left her alone and unprotected, her boss contributed to a work environment that undermined her sense of safety and security in her job.

What Carrie needed instead was a Joash. When the Boss called Joash's son, Gideon, to lead the nation of Israel, He also instructed him to clean up his own family's loyalty issues first by destroying his father's altars to other gods. Gideon took care of the problem in the middle of the night because he was afraid of his family and the men of the town (Judges 6:1-32).

Sure enough, when they awoke the next morning, found their idols and altars demolished, a new altar built, and discovered who did it, the men of the town demanded that Joash bring his own son forth to face the death penalty. However, despite the loss of his own sacred things, Joash protected his son from the hostile crowd.

> Employers have a responsibility to look out for, backup, defend, safeguard, shield, and warn their employees.

"If Baal really is a god," Joash responded, "he can defend himself when someone breaks down his altar" (Judges 6:31).

Carrie needed that kind of response. Yet, when the hostile crowd angry about the threats to their sacred altar confronted Carrie's boss, instead of protecting her, he turned her over to the crowd and joined them in their cause against her.

No Thanks

Matt accepted a full-time position as a youth director at a church. His program area exploded under his leadership and the church experienced an amazing season of growth in conjunction with his work and that of other staff members.

Because of the growth, the church leadership decided to expand the facilities. However, due to budget constraints and the need to find additional funds to help pay for the facility expansions, the leadership decided to cut several full-time positions to part-time. Even worse, significant changes in job duties and expectations did NOT accompany the abrupt change, meaning workers were expected to soldier on and pony up for the team.

As a result, most of the directly affected staff members ended up leaving shortly thereafter. The church experienced membership and program decline partly due to the staff vacancies, and the building project took longer than expected and had to be revised from the original plan due to reduction in income and reduced needs for additional space.

Although the ministry's leaders could have and should have protected their employees, their actions left many feeling betrayed, exposed, and vulnerable.

Walls and Gates

When people feel threatened or unprotected, they tend to experience pain, anger, and a sense of vulnerability that is not conducive to fostering a healthy workplace environment.

Furthermore, these feelings of uneasiness can heighten workplace tensions. Trivial things explode into massive things. Words and actions that normally pass by like a gentle breeze suddenly erupt into full-blown storms. Instead of tiptoeing joyfully through tulips, office interactions turn into dangerous attempts to navigate through minefields.

Kings and armies, walls and gates, keys and contracts – and exceptional bosses – provide protection.

18

Provide Supervision

Wherever one falls on the spectrum of attempting to define differences between leaders and managers, the underlying matter of contention involves how to move people with varied backgrounds, personalities, skills, and styles to work together effectively. Most organizational processes involve some sort of supervision. This requires healthy communication, which may vary widely depending on the boss and the team. Assistive tools that can help people better understand one another and improve teamwork include instruments such as the DISC[1] behavioral style model that depicts primary behavioral types in a circle divided into four quadrants – Dominant, Inspiring, Supportive, and Cautious.

---

[1] The DISC model is rooted in research published in Dr. William Moulton Marston's 1928 book, *Emotions of Normal People*. A lawyer and psychologist, Marston invented the first functional lie detector polygraph, outlined the basis of the DISC model for emotions and behavior of normal people, authored self-help books and created the *Wonder Woman* comic. He defined the four quadrants of personality as Dominance, Influence, Steadiness, and Compliance. By 1948, industrial psychologist Walter V. Clarke had devised a personality profile instrument using Marston's theories. Published in 1956, his "Activity Vector Analysis" utilized a checklist of adjectives asking people to mark descriptors they identified as true of themselves that placed them on a quadrant of four data factors he labeled Aggressive, Sociable, Stable and Avoidant.

The Myers-Briggs Type Indicator (MBTI)[2] is another tool that identifies 16 personality types in four-letter combinations comprised from rankings of four dichotomies of personality: Extraversion (E) vs. Introversion (I), Sensing (S) vs. Intuition (N), Thinking (T) vs. Feeling (F), and Judging (J) vs. Perception (P).

> *Methods of supervising may vary widely, while core needs remain somewhat constant.*

These and other personality tests seek to identify and explain observed ranges of styles of thinking and feeling that tend to correspond with certain ways of behaving. With more than 7 billion people[3] on planet earth, millions of cultures (from family, club, school, regional, state, and national to corporate, religious, social, and team, etc.), and more than 7000 languages,[4] methods of supervising may vary widely, while core needs remain somewhat constant. Elements of appropriate, balanced, and effective oversight seem to include the following:

- Clear articulation of purpose, vision, mission, plans
- Corresponding correction and guidance
- Allowance of expression
- Permission to negotiate

---

[2] The Myers Briggs Type Indicator (MBTI) originated with Carl Gustav Jung's research and 1921 publication of the book, *Psychological Types*, in which he identified four ways in which people experience the world: Sensation, Intuition, Feeling, and Thinking. In 1962, Katherine Cook Brigg and her daughter, Isabel Briggs Myers, utilized Jung's theories to create and publish the first MBTI survey.

[3] "U.S. and World Population Clock" (Census.gov/popclock).

[4] "Ethnologue: Languages of the World," Gary F. Simons and Charles D. Fennig (eds.), Twentieth edition, 2017. Dallas, Texas: SIL International (Ethnologue.com).

Clear Articulation of Purpose Vision, Mission, Plans

God clearly articulated His purpose vision, mission, and plans to *Noah* regarding building an ark (Genesis 6-9).

God clearly articulated His plan to destroy Sodom and Gomorrah to *Abraham*, after first considering whether to hide from him what was about to happen. Their engaging interaction after God shared the plan seems to evidence a respectful attitude toward Abraham, as does their debate on where to draw the line for destruction (Genesis 18-19).

God clearly articulated exacting and numerous details to *Moses* about the exodus, the journey to and anticipated life in the Promised Land, the Law, and much more.

Isaiah, Jeremiah, Daniel, and *other prophets* received clear visions and plans about what to do in preparation for, during, and after exile. Daniel spent the rest of his life in Babylon after his forced relocation there as a young man. When he understood from Jeremiah's writings that the exile was scheduled for 70 years, Daniel asked God to reconsider, but then accepted the explanation and lived out his life of service to God faithfully in the capital city of the foreign country of Babylon (Daniel 9).

David informed his son, *Solomon,* that God gave him plans for the temple, even though he was not to build it.

> "All this I have in writing from the hand of the Lord upon me, and he gave me understanding in all the details of the plan" (I Chronicles 28:19).

Thus, in the scriptures, God models this critical element of supervising – clearly articulating vision, mission, and plans so people understand what is ahead and their role in it.

Corresponding Correction and Guidance

When God hired and provided plans and parameters, He did not then usually leave people alone with no additional interactions, like in deism (the idea that God created the world, wound it up like a clock, and has since left it alone).[5]

Rather, God actively supervised by engaging as needed in instigation, implementation, and follow through, not by intruding overbearingly into every single action. Even when everything was set up perfectly and still went awry, God's supervision seemed aimed toward refinement, clarification, and feedback adjustments, as well as punishments typically used as teaching moments.

God once met with *Moses and his siblings* to address their rivalry. Aaron and Miriam were older and jealous of their younger brother. God admonished them for their selfish grumbling and made it clear that He made Moses boss, Moses did not pick himself. God wanted their trio to work together – each in their appropriate place – and the meeting helped recalibrate their mutual understanding of each one's individual placements and priorities (Numbers 12).

When *Moses* almost received glory and honor by simply speaking to a rock to miraculously produce water for his community, he acted dishonorably in the moment his Boss planned to honor him. Moses called people names, took credit for the upcoming miracle, and hit the rock, twice. These actions earned him a reprimand that included banishment from entering the Promised Land (Numbers 20:1-13).

---

[5] The theology that God created the universe according to scientific laws but does not interfere in its daily operation was articulated in Voltaire's 1734 work, *Traité de Métaphysique*. He likened God to a watchmaker who designed the universe, set it in motion, and refrains from interference thereafter, yet his presence remains visible in all creation.

David received a strong rebuke after he sent his men into battle one spring and he stayed behind and strayed with a neighbor, who happened to be the wife of one of his most trusted soldiers. Though David tried to cover his initial sin of adultery with deceit, manipulation, and then murder, God confronted and corrected him through the prophet Nathan, and punished the couple for their sin (II Samuel 11-12).

Nebuchadnezzar received admonition for his arrogance and pride, which led to his banishment and a departure from his throne for seven years. However, he learned about humility, the dangers of pride, and the source of true power and authority (Daniel 4).

> *God actively supervised by engaging as needed in instigation, implementation, and follow through, not by intruding overbearingly into every single action.*

While some employees need no correction or guidance, most will either need or seek clarifications to stay on track, and usually, the sooner the better. Ecclesiastes 8:11 highlights the importance of responding quickly to errant situations, "When the sentence for a crime is not quickly carried out, the hearts of the people are filled with schemes to do wrong." Public correction and punishment often provided opportunities for indirect learning for the larger community, not just the individuals involved.

Scripture does record evidence that failing to adequately admonish can cause more problems. Consider Aaron's failure to correct the people who wanted to make gods (Exodus 32), and David's failure to address the errant behavior of his sons Amnon and Absalom (II Samuel 13).

Allowance of Expression

Did God allow employees to voice feelings and thoughts? The recurring Hebrew complaints in the wilderness eventually aroused God's anger and resulted in punishment (Numbers 11:1). However, this should not lead anyone to think God allowed zero expressions of anger, angst, discontent, or inquiry. One group's repeated excess and punishment does not reveal the whole pattern of God's supervisory actions.

Shortly after *Moses* first confronted Pharaoh, and then Pharaoh made things worse for the Hebrews, Moses went back to God and complained. "Why, Lord, why have you brought trouble on this people? Is this why you sent me? Ever since I went to Pharaoh to speak in your name, he has brought trouble on this people, and you have not rescued your people at all" (Exodus 5:22-23). The Boss did not shut him up or shut him down. Rather, God clearly rearticulated His purpose, promises and plan, and encouraged Moses to stay in the game.

When Moses later complained about being overworked, God responded by providing him with new employees to help him (Numbers 11:10-15).

When *Elijah* expressed his fear, questioned his zeal, and asserted his loneliness, God responded by giving him food and rest, arranging a personal meeting, offering him hope, and providing an updated strategic plan (I Kings 19).

When *Jonah* expressed displeasure and anger toward God, the Boss provided for his needs and engaged him in discussion to talk things out (Jonah 4).

When *David* expressed his fear and anger about Uzzah's death after the man touched the Ark of the Covenant to keep it from falling off an ox cart, God did not punish David, but let him ponder it long enough to change his tactics (2 Samuel 6).

Permission to Negotiate

In the earlier mention recounting God's visit to *Abraham* on His way to conduct an on-site review before destroying Sodom and Gomorrah, recall that God allowed for discussion concerning what was about to happen. When the Boss shared inside information, Abraham did not like what he heard. In fact, he thought God's plans seemed unfair.

He then respectfully offered his opinions, which included potential variables providing for the possibility that the Boss would not follow through on His plans. Although his negotiations ultimately did not change the outcome, Abraham did his best to try and protect people so corrupt that not even ten righteous people lived in the entire city. Abraham modeled good debate manners by engaging respectfully, and God revealed a model willingness to engage in reflective and responsive negotiations up to a certain point (Genesis 18-19).

When *Moses* balked at God's initial call, God allowed negotiations that showed a willingness to allow for certain accommodations (Exodus 3-4).

When God's frustration with His employees led Him to announce that He would prefer to just kill them all, he allowed Moses to negotiate on the people's behalf, as well as on behalf of God's own reputation.

"I have seen these people," the Lord said to Moses, "and they are a stiff-necked people. Now leave me alone so that my anger may burn against them and that I may destroy them. Then I will make you into a great nation." However, Moses sought the favor of the Lord his God. "Lord," he said, "why should your anger burn against your people, whom you brought out of

Egypt with great power and a mighty hand? Why should the Egyptians say, 'It was with evil intent that he brought them out, to kill them in the mountains and to wipe them off the face of the earth'? Turn from your fierce anger; relent and do not bring disaster on your people. Remember your servants Abraham, Isaac and Israel, to whom you swore by your own self: 'I will make your descendants as numerous as the stars in the sky and I will give your descendants all this land I promised them, and it will be their inheritance forever.'" Then the Lord relented and did not bring on his people the disaster he had threatened (Exodus 32:9-14).

When *David* initiated a census – perhaps out of pride – it angered God so much that He offered David three options for punishment. The one David chose resulted in 70,000 of his citizens dying in a three-day plague. During the plague, David initiated a negotiation to stop the plague, and that resulted in the purchase of the land where Solomon later built the first Jewish temple in Jerusalem (2 Samuel 24).

When God told the prophet *Ezekiel* to embody the upcoming siege of Jerusalem by laying down on his side for over a year tied up with ropes, He informed Ezekiel that he would need to cook his food over human excrement during that time. However, Ezekiel balked and reiterated his lifetime commitment to cleanliness and godliness, even in his diet. Then God responded kindly, "I will let you bake your bread over cow manure instead of human excrement" (Ezekiel 4). Like Ezekiel, maybe your job comes with poo, too, but the kind of poo might be negotiable in some cases.

Reflection

Joseph Louis Barrow, better known as "Joe Louis," held the world's heavyweight championship belt from 1937 until 1949. He is widely considered one of boxing's all-time greats.

However, one of Joe's greatest victories may have occurred when he encouraged a troubled teen named Charles "Doc" Broadus to pursue the art of boxing, telling the errant youngster, "You will be a great one day."

Doc went on to achieve an amateur record of 100-0, and only lost his first pro fight after 22 wins. He eventually joined the Air Force, served in two wars, and retired as sergeant to run a gym and serve as a Lyndon B. Johnson Job Corps Counselor in Pleasanton, California.

However, one of Doc's greatest victories may have occurred when he left watching TV one night to answer a call about a melee in one of the Job Corps dorms.

"Somebody said, 'There's a young man here trying to beat up everybody,'" Broadus recalled. "I go over there and find that this 16-year-old kid, George Foreman, had taken the door off the hinges, beat up on a kid and thrown him out the window."

A native of Marshall, Texas who grew up in Houston's rough Fifth Ward district, Foreman was a 9th grade dropout, self-proclaimed thug, and gang member. He had only recently attempted to escape his troubled life after seeing Johnny Unitas on a public service announcement asking young men to join the job corps.

Doc, a 5'5" martial arts expert initially challenged the much taller brawler to pick on somebody his own size, but then decided to step into a supervisory role by inviting Foreman, "Come on, big fella. Let's walk and talk."

While the other Job Corps counselors wanted to send the troublemaker to the nearby state prison, Broadus dissuaded them and encouraged Foreman, "You're big enough and ugly enough to be a fighter. Let's get on down to the gym."

Under Broadus' supervision – wherein he cast a clear vision, corrected and guided as needed, allowed Foreman to express and work through his angst and discontent, and then the two negotiated various issues – Foreman advanced rapidly. Within two years, he won Olympic gold in the heavyweight boxing division in Mexico City in 1968 after only his 25th amateur fight. He continued on to win his first 27 professional fights before winning his first world championship by defeating "Smokin" Joe Frazier in Kingston, Jamaica on January 22, 1973.

Shortly thereafter, Foreman lost his title to Muhammad Ali in "Rumble in the Jungle" title bout in Kinshasa, Zaire on October 30, 1974 in his only defeat by knockout in his entire professional career. He then retired at age 35 after losing an attempt to regain the title from Jimmy Young in March 1977, became a non-denominational Christian minister, and led the George Foreman Youth and Community Center in Houston.

However, Foreman returned on November 5, 1994 after a ten-year hiatus and at age 45 to become world's oldest heavyweight champion in history at age 45. He retired again in 1997 with a professional record of 76 wins (68 by knockout) and only 5 losses.

He then embarked on a successful career as a minister, HBO sports broadcaster, and entrepreneur. He sold rights to his name and image to Grill manufacturer Salton, Inc. for $137.5 million in cash and stock in 1999. He has successfully launched other ventures that include a clothing line, books, and a reality show featuring his family. The International Boxing Hall of Fame inducted Foreman on June 8, 2003.

Thus, the chain of supervisory influence through Joe Louis and then Doc Broadus helped shape Foreman's 6'3" and 200+ pounds into a positive force that continues to positively influence others to this day.

Foreman explains his continuing the chain of influence through providing supervision this way, "I started a youth center in Houston. The kids would come in and want to learn to box; they wanted to tear up the world, beat up the world. I'd try to show them they didn't need anger. They didn't need all that killing instinct they'd read about. You can be a human being and pursue boxing as a sport."[6]

---

[6] Compiled from "The Official Website of George Foreman" at GeorgeForeman.com; "George Foreman Biography.com," Biography.com Editors, A&E Television Networks, Biography.com; and "George Foreman Quotes," BrainyQuote.com.

19

Provide Training

By the time the Lord called *Moses* to lead the Hebrew people, Moses had 80 years of foundational training and experience in what would prove to be needed critical skills.

Following his infant rescue from the Nile River by Pharaoh's daughter, he lived in Pharaoh's own household for 40 years, and "was educated in all the wisdom of the Egyptians and was powerful in speech and action" (Acts 7:22). He spent another 40 years as a foreign exchange student living and working as a shepherd in Midian.

Thus, by the time Moses rose to a position of leadership, he had 40 years of training in education and politics, as well as 40 years of training in birthing, providing for, protecting, and shepherding flocks across desert and mountain terrains.

Even so, he continued to receive additional, on-the-job training throughout his next 40 years of employment. God trained him directly as things happened and questions arose, and indirectly as he and other leaders and various groups of people worked through issues. The Lord also provided continuing education through people, such as Moses' own father-in-law (Exodus 18).

David received years of training as a shepherd before Samuel showed up at his home to anoint him. David then enrolled in a work-study program for King Saul as a warrior, musician, and personal aide prior to ascending to the throne. His 40-year reign included additional years of continuing education through various advisors, prophets, and priests.

Daniel and his friends originally caught their captors' attention due to their apparent good looks, aptitude for learning, and other abilities and qualifications. However, they rose to leadership among their people and the Babylonian kingdom through a journey that included three years of training in the language and literature of the Babylonians, and successfully passing their comprehensive exams and other tests along the way (Daniel 1-6). Daniel's continuing education program involved dreams, visions, and special guest lectures, presentations, and training sessions by God, the archangel Gabriel, and perhaps other angels (Daniel 7-12).

The Right Recipe

After 25 years of baking homemade cheesecakes in her Detroit, Michigan basement, Evelyn Overton and her husband, Oscar, packed up and moved to Los Angeles, California in 1972 with $10,000 to open a little cheesecake bakery. In 1978, their son, David, opened a restaurant in Beverly Hills to showcase his mother's cheesecakes. Ten minutes after opening, the 78 seats of The Cheesecake Factory were filled with hungry customers, and business flourished.

Over the last four decades, the unique eatery has grown to include more than 200 locations offering 50 delicious desserts and more than 250 menu selections with 70 sauces and dressings – all freshly handmade, in-house, every day.

The $2.2 billion dollar per year business[1] ranked No. 1 in Casual-dining Restaurants in the *Nation's Restaurant News'* 2016 Consumer Picks survey[2], made the *Fortune's* 2017 "100 Best Companies to Work For,"[3] and CEO David Overton debuted at number 34 (coincidently the same number of cheesecakes on The Cheesecake Factory menu) on Glassdoor's 2017 Highest Rated CEO list, where employees gave him a 93% leadership approval rating based on over two million anonymous company reviews.[4]

So, what keeps bringing in nearly 10 million people per month[5] to eat at The Cheesecake Factory restaurants?

"We've changed the menu twice a year, every year, for 40 years," says Overton. "That's what keeps people interested. And it keeps us current. We don't rest on our laurels."[6]

Their 40,000 employees would most likely agree, since they help manage the enterprise, meet and greet, prepare and serve the food, and keep up with the bi-annual changes in the extensive menu selections and the abundant ingredients. But, how do these employees keep current, and why are so many so pleased with their boss and their company?

"We believe we have one of the most comprehensive training programs in the industry. We offer tools ranging from a state-of-the-art online Learning Management System to

---

[1] "Revenue of The Cheesecake Factory from 2009 to 2017 (in billion U.S. dollars)," February 2018, Statista.com

[2] "Consumer Picks 2016: Casual-Dining Results," 4 April 2016, *Nation's Restaurant News*, NRN.com.

[3] "The 100 Best Companies to Work For," 2017, Fortune.com.

[4] "Highest Rated CEOs 2017 Employees' Choice," GlassDoor.com.

[5] "Number of people who visited The Cheesecake Factory within the last 30 days in the United States from spring 2011 to spring 2017 (in millions)," Statista.com.

[6] "2017 Golden Chain Award winner: David Overton: Cheesecake Factory CEO's recipe for success: 'Break all the rules'," Ron Ruggless, 1 October 2017, *Nation's Restaurant News*, NRN.com.

extensive and continuous restaurant management training and development, including mentoring and coaching."[7]

New employees begin with a comprehensive multi-week training program, and the company provides 320 hours of professional development and training per year to full-time salaried staff and 150 hours to full-time hourly staff.[8]

Overton points out that their extensive menu essentially requires staff to serve as tour guides, not just servers. Plus, the consistent use of perfected systems, technology, and the intentional development of their employees enables guests to have consistently memorable dining experiences.[9]

Employee training includes various engaging and creative use of technologies such as leaderboards and iPhone apps. A knowledge-sharing portal enables employees to upload videos of solutions to typical restaurant problems, and videos shared in the online staff "Video Cafe" include comments, ratings, and blogs. The highest rated videos are shown on the leaderboard to make learning more fun and inviting.

> *By the time an employee has played several times, they have memorized the proper recipe.*

For even more good times and training, The Cheesecake Factory created an iPhone app that teaches the recipes for "glamburgers." Rather than ask employees to memorize ingredients, they play a challenging "build the burger" iPhone game that shows a hamburger bun and meat, toppings, and

[7] "Building An Amazing Place To Work," TheCheesecakeFactory.com/Corporate-social-responsibility/culture, March 2018.

[8] Reviews.greatplacetowork.com/the-cheesecake-factory-incorporated, March 2018.

[9] "Questions for...Cheesecake Factory's David Overton," Caroline Fairchild, 16 January 2014, Fortune.com.

condiments falling from the sky, and employees must catch them in the right order to earn points. Burgers keep coming in increasing in speed and in point value as the game progresses. Successful completion of one level allows players to move to the next level with changing burger orders that require arranging the ingredients in different orders and combinations. After mastering each level, gamers move to the next level in such a way that by the time an employee has played several times, they have memorized the proper recipe for each burger.[10]

Past evidence reveals that the pay-off of spending $2,000 per person per year has translated to sales of $1,000 per square foot – more than twice the industry average – and an employee retention rate of about 15 percent better than the national average.[11]

Spending vs. Investing

In a national study of workplace learning practices and outcomes of 540 U.S. Corporations conducted and published in 1998 by The American Society for Training and Development (ASTD),[12] those investing at least 6% of payroll on training and continuing education had 57% higher sales per employee and a 37% higher gross profit per employee than those that spent minimal amounts. The best results came from companies training at least 86% of employees and complimenting classroom sessions with Internet resources,

---

[10] "'Gamifying' Training [With The Cheesecake Factory]," 15 June 2012, Nicci Strong, EnGaming.wordpress.com.

[11] "Cheesecake Factory Cooks Up a Rigorous Employee Training Program," Gina Ruiz, 3 May 3006, Workforce.com. "

[12] "The 1998 ASTD State of the Industry Report," Laurie J. Bassi and Mark E. Van Buren, *Training and Development*, January 1998, pp. 21-49.

webinars and other computer-based training opportunities. Curtis Plott, president of ASTD at the time, announced at an international conference that the study provided "concrete evidence showing that companies who invest more heavily in workplace training are more successful and profitable." [13]

In the ASTD's initial report in 1998, firms investing $1,500 per employee as compared to those investing only $125 per employee averaged a 24% higher gross profit margin and a 218% higher revenue per employee. Among industries included 19 years later in the annual "2017 State of the Industry" report, the renamed Association for Talent Development (ATD) reported average expenditures of $1,273 per employee for 34.1 average formal learning hours in 2016. [14]

> "You don't build a business. You build people, and people build the business."
>
> "The only thing worse than training your people and losing them is not training them and keeping them."
>
> Zig Ziglar

In a 2012 study of more than 1,200 employees, nearly 95% of young high achievers actively looked for other jobs during their first employment stint and left their companies, on average, after 28 months. Young managers reported valuing company development efforts, such as placement in high-visibility positions and increasing responsibilities, but also reported a lack of formal training, mentoring, and coaching. Ironically, companies reluctant to train workers also seem

---

[13] "Research shows that training employees pays off with profits," Jack Warkenthien, 6 January 2002, *Memphis Business Journal.*

[14] "2017 State of the Industry," Association for Talent Development, 2017, ATD Research, td.org.

more prone to lose motivated employees dissatisfied with the lack of training opportunities and investment.[15]

Though some believe tuition assistance and continuing education increases risks of employee departure, companies that view training programs as investments with a "high value" to their overall enterprise believe participants are more likely to stay with the organization.[16]

"Development planning doesn't have to be elaborate or costly," notes author, Forbes.com contributor, and founder and principal of Howling Wolf Management Training, Victor Lipman. "At its core it's mostly a matter of good managers taking the person-to-person time to understand their employees...recognizing their skills and needs...and guiding them to fill in the gaps. If it's done well, the payoff can be substantial in terms of long-term loyalty. If it's not, the costs can be substantial in terms of long-term talent.[17]

Across fourteen years of research between 1998 and 2012 involving more than 17,000 responses from employees in a variety of occupations, at all levels, in organizations of all sizes, in a wide range of industries and market sectors, researchers Beverly Kaye and Sharon Jordan-Evans sought insights into what keeps workers in and committed to an organization. Their research focused on several questions, such as: What keeps an employee with an employer? What keeps talent fully engaged on the job? Why do people stay, both physically and psychologically?

---

[15] "Why Top Young Managers Are in a Nonstop Job Hunt," Monika Hamori, Jie Cao, Burak Koyuncu, July-August 2012, *Harvard Business Review*, HBR.org.

[16] "Tuition Assistance Programs – Key Findings and Maturity Model," 12 November 2012, WHATWORKS Brief, Bersin & Associates.

[17] "Why Employee Development Is Important, Neglected And Can Cost You Talent," Victor Lipman, 29 January 2013, Forbes.com.

Among the 20 "Stay Factors" Kaye and Jordan-Evans identified in their white paper "What Matters Most?"[18] as top drivers of engaging and retaining talent, three factors remained consistently among the top five:

- Exciting and meaningful work challenges

- Supportive management and a good boss

- Career growth, learning and development

Disney Institute Vice-President and General Manager, Jeff James, writes, "What we've observed through our work over the past 30 years is that too many organizations tend to underestimate the amount of support people need in achieving desired levels of performance."[19]

James outlines three important training opportunities employers have that can send powerful, positive messages:

1. *Onboarding* – including introductions to organizational history, purpose, culture, and quality standards, as well as "how-to" training.
2. *Transitioning Positions* – including reinforcing values and vision along with reinforcement of skills and training in new skills.
3. *Continuous Learning & Development* – including opportunities to further one's skills and leadership effectiveness.

---

[18] "What Matters Most? A White Paper About Organizational Stay Factors: Update Findings," Beverly Kaye and Sharon Jordan-Evans, October 2012, Career Systems International & Jordan Evans Group.

[19] "Optional or Operational – The Case For Great Training," Jeff James, 26 February 2018, *Disney Institute* Talking Point: The *Disney Institute* Blog, DisneyInstitute.com.

Employers also note the crucial importance of recognizing lifelong learners. Employees who demonstrate ambition, leadership, and seem desirous of remaining aware of industry trends and advancements tend to benefit from more proactive development from their leaders.[20]

"Those who do have the opportunity to continue to learn and develop tend to be more engaged, more productive, and more likely to stay with a company," says James.[21]

Not everyone can, or needs to be, a Moses, a David, or a Daniel, and not every employee needs to memorize the ingredients of 250 menu items, reach the highest levels of the Glamburger game, or work for the Magic Kingdom. However, most employees need and benefit from intentional growth processes to help them better do what they were hired to do, advance and expand their repertoire of knowledge and skills, increase their confidence, and experience new opportunities.

---

[20] "Lifelong Education and Labor Market Needs: An examination of how ongoing learning benefits the society, the corporation and the individual," *The EvoLLLution*, July 2012, Destiny Solutions, Inc.

[21] (Ibid, footnote 19)

Section Three

Firing Well

20

Introduction

T he Director wondered if this applicant was an answer to prayer. Although her posted job opening resulted in an overwhelming number of responses, none yet appeared to meet the specific criteria necessary for this position. However, immediately after praying for clarity, wisdom, and the right candidate to come along, the administrator noticed a job application stuck under the bottom of a pile on her desk.

The apparently overlooked application stood out. In fact, everything about the applicant shouted, "I'm perfect for this job! I am the one you want! Hire me!" The ensuing phone calls, emails, interview, and references all seemed to confirm that this, indeed, might be the elusive, but ideal, candidate. Due to the urgency of filling the position, the Director offered the candidate the provisional opportunity to begin work immediately, with the understanding that a formal contract would follow a successful background check.

The recruit did suggest that her background check might be problematic due to an old case of identity theft, and she produced documentation appearing to verify her claim.

Sure enough, the candidate's background check did not go through quickly. In fact, after several resubmissions, the background check came back indeterminate.

"This person does not exist," the agency replied.

In the meantime, the recruit leapt into action. Her manner appeared pleasing to others on her team, and clients initially responded well to her work.

However, an issue arose within the first two weeks. One of her clients said one thing happened, but the recruit insisted she said nothing of the sort, or ever would, explaining, "I am not that kind of person."

> *Some employments need to come to a decisive end initiated by an employer.*

Shortly thereafter, another issue arose with several other clients and their associates. They claimed one thing, but the recruit denied their claims based on supposedly obvious collusion and, again, appealed to her impeccable character.

Around the same time, a staff associate confided to the Director something the recruit said to her in private. This statement independently corroborated the clients' accounts of what happened, since, at the time, the staff associate had no knowledge or awareness of the other incidents.

From the beginning, the Director discussed each circumstance with the recruit and each person involved. She also observed the new employee in action on the job. Unfortunately, the gulf between consensus among others and observed reality – and the new recruit's interpretation of reality – seemed ever widening. By this point, the Director realized the potential hire might prove more problematic than providential.

Finally, the background check came back – with several wildly waving flags. The person did exist, and her fingerprints matched her confirmed identity and corroborated with official documents. She also had a confirmed record with a list of eye-opening convictions that included running a brothel (yes, this is a true story!) and various other behaviors that generally indicate questionable character, quite the opposite of her sanctimonious claims of purity she voiced in her application, interviews, and personal interactions.

Thus, three weeks in, the Director realized this recruit was probably NOT an answer to prayer. Instead of completing the hiring process, the Director reversed course and terminated the almost employee. Not surprisingly, the person's vitriolic response to the Director's actions more closely matched the personality suggested from her legally recorded past than the angelic character she claimed.

Firing Well

Unfortunately, and for many different reasons, some employments need to come to a decisive end initiated by an employer. Equally unfortunate, some employers execute the firing process poorly, and occasionally, terminated employees do not respond well to getting cut from their team.

> *How firings occur often harm and hurt more than **why**.*

Some of the most grievous employment wounds in many people's lives relate to either firing someone or getting fired. Some hate both, and few like aspects of either. However, there are better ways and positive possibilities.

So, how should firings occur if and when they must? What appropriate protocols, processes, and practices can help mitigate potential problems? Firing someone is a significant action and requires thoughtful intentionality regardless of circumstances and whether a person likes the task of terminating someone else's employment. *How* firings occur often harm and hurt more than *why*.

The chapters ahead review six circumstances where the Boss hired, and then later fired, one or more employees. In one case, God even rehired someone previously fired.

If you have ever had to fire someone, or may need to fire someone in the future, some of these insights may prove beneficial.

21

Case One – Adam and Eve

T he first few chapters of Genesis include the account of God's hiring and kind of firing of the first-ever human employees named in the Bible – Adam and Eve.

The couple received clear parameters that included a job description: work and take care of the property, rule over the animals, be fruitful and multiply. The Boss specified the location of their employment (the Garden of Eden), the personnel roster (Adam and Eve), and gave clear provisions (every seed-bearing plant and every tree that has fruit with seed in it). However, the Boss also distinctly noted a single, specific limitation with clearly defined consequences.

"You are free to eat from any tree in the garden, but you must not eat from the tree of the knowledge of good and evil, for when you do eat of it you will surely die" (Genesis 2:16-17).

At some point in time – the textual account does not offer any details relative to how much time passed – the couple directly disobeyed the Boss's instructions.

The first impression as the Boss arrived on the scene indicates peace, described as God "walking in the garden in the cool of the day." But, like many have experienced when everything seems fine and calm, things were about to go awry.

The couple initially hid in fear as the Boss approached. This abnormal behavior apparently raised a signal flag to the Boss, as such actions often do.

How many times have the approaching footsteps of a boss generated fear, worry, or some other unhealthy thought or feeling? In healthy situations, not a single person changes their actions in any way due to either the presence or absence of their boss. Without fear to taint feelings, or following through on temptations to deceive, people can rest fully in truth and trust. Inward and outward reactions when one hears the footsteps of a boss approaching can provide helpful measurements of actions, character, and relationship. In this first couple's case, the Lord's behavioral monitoring meters pinged to red.

When questioned, Adam admitted knowledge he should not have known. Again, something abnormal. God knew that awareness could only have been possible if Adam and/or Eve had transgressed the single prohibition. Adam's explanation may not have intended to reveal the truth, but inadvertently did so when questioned.

A wife once wanted to buy her husband a gift from the mall. She needed him to drop her off but did not want him to know which store she planned to go to since that might give away the nature of the gift. However, when he asked where she preferred him to drop her off, she replied, "I don't know where in the bookstore it is." Giant hint, and completely unintentional!

Investigators know that people often drop clues unaware during interrogation. Astute bosses learn to pay attention because people often reveal truth inadvertently even during carefully crafted lies. People also attempt to deceive via distraction, which leads to another factor in this situation – blame.

The Boss's confrontation launched a blame game. Adam blamed God AND Eve ("the woman you gave me"), and she blamed the serpent. Again, this abnormal behavior provided another indication of misdeeds.

Seeking to avoid personal responsibility – blaming others, detracting, distorting, distracting, hiding, procrastinating – all seem a consequence of disobedience from the very beginning. Needless and prolonged waste, damage, and destruction still result from such behavior.

Upon discovering and confirming the violation of their terms of contract through observation, interrogation, and interpretation, the Boss began to fulfill the promise of proportionate consequences (Genesis 3). Notice that the Boss addressed the employees directly, asked questions, sought to interpret the situation accurately, requested clarification, made decisions, and acted on them. He seems to have fired them quickly, with some immediate consequences, along with other consequences that occurred over time.

God tailored specific consequences to everyone involved, including the third party who intervened. Eve's consequences included painful childbirth and patriarchal rule. Adam's consequences included painful toil and the necessity of cultivating sustenance. The serpent's consequences included the curse of crawling in the dust, enmity with Eve and between both of their offspring, and eventual defeat in battle.

There were also general, collective consequences that had wide impact far beyond their own time and circumstance. Just as a stone tossed into a still pond makes waves far beyond the point of entry, singular actions can have wide consequences seemingly far out of proportion to their initial happenstance. This happens in community when people, organizations, time, and history are in relationship. Although the couple's specific curses affected them specifically, the curses also affected endless waves of their descendants.

> *The Boss fired these employees WITH benefits.*

It is interesting to note that the Boss fired these employees WITH benefits. Though Adam and Eve were banished from the Garden of Eden, the Boss also gave them immediate provision (clothes), as well as protection (banishment and a flaming sword to bar them from returning and eating from the Tree of Life and living eternally).

The provision of clothes makes sense, but how did banishment and a guard against reentry protect them? The Boss explains the necessity. With the introduction of problems, the worst thing that could happen would be for the couple to be able to live forever in such a compromised condition. Although painful, death trumped forever existing in a state of perpetual imperfection.

Firing guidelines, based on this case, might include immediate termination upon confirmation of a major, well-defined infraction, as well as an option to fire with benefits, i.e. provision and protection. In today's business world, post-firing benefits are often called a "severance package."

Guidelines for firing:

1. Direct conversation
2. Seek clarification and accurate interpretation of the circumstance(s) and issue(s)
3. Detail immediate and long-term consequences
4. Act with speed, especially if danger lurks

Employees should:

1. Receive clear warning ahead of time
2. Evidence transgression
3. Expect repercussion

Bosses should be:

1. Clear and consistent
2. Willing to follow through on promises
3. Willing to consider gracious, undeserved assistance in some cases

The ensuing biblical chapters depict the Boss's continued relationship with the fired employees afterwards, as well as with their children (Genesis 4). Most firings often result in either no, or at least extremely limited, future communication between the firer and fired. However, this case evidences a continued relationship, of sorts. Some might point out that there were no other people on the planet at the time, which is not our circumstance, so this case could be an exception.

Even so, firing someone may not always lead to the ending of a relationship, but these types of circumstances will often and understandably change relationships significantly.

Reflection

Born the third child of a Jewish stationery business owner and French mother in New York in 1948, Frank William Abagnale, Jr. launched his early career in counterfeiting at age 15 with his father's credit card. Troubled by his parent's divorce and his own fraudulent actions, he ran away from home and between ages 16 and 21 wrote $2.5 million in bad checks worldwide while notably impersonating a Pan Am airline pilot, a doctor, and a lawyer (he passed the bar on the third try after studying for 7 months). He quit scamming and tried to settle in Montpelier, France before an old girlfriend saw his picture on a wanted poster and turned him in to authorities. Following his convictions, he served time in prisons in France, Sweden, and the United States. The U.S. government offered parole after serving 5 of his 12-year sentence in Petersburg, Virginia in exchange for assisting the FBI with fraud prevention.

Abagnale went on to become a world-renowned expert on check swindling, document fraud, embezzlement, and forgery, and started his own company, Abagnale & Associates, to help corporations, financial institutions, and government agencies around the world combat white collar crime and fraud. Abagnale served as an FBI consultant for decades and refused to accept payment for any of his government work. The FBI recovered $2 million of the funds Abagnale stole, and he later paid back the remaining $500,000. He lectures at the FBI Academy and field offices, is a faculty member for the Department of Justice's National Advocacy Center (NAC), and provides consulting services for the thousands of financial institutions, corporations and law enforcement agencies that use his fraud prevention programs.

Joseph Shea, an FBI agent who died in 2005, relentlessly helped track down and convict Abagnale. Even so, Abagnale and Shea became lifelong friends following his arrest and convictions. In a 2008 interview with *Computer Dealer News* Staff at Computerworld's Storage Networking World conference, Abagnale answered why.

"He and I were friends for 30 years; he died at the age of 88 just about a year ago. He was a great help up until his death. I watched his two daughters grow up and get married; I attended their weddings. He watched my children grow up. He was obviously a big part of my life in getting me out of prison and getting me to work with the government. He was someone who saw that I had something to offer and he was very big on helping me do that. I think when he started out, he thought I was some master criminal and he was going to catch me, but when he came to the realization that I was just a kid and I was a runaway, being a father, he had a lot more compassion."[1]

Exaggerated and fictionalized accounts of his crime spree served as the basis for Abagnale's book[2], as well as the film, *Catch Me If You Can* (2002), directed by Steven Spielberg and starring Leonardo DiCaprio as Abagnale and Tom Hanks as the FBI agent in pursuit.[3]

[1] "Frank Abagnale breaks his silence," CDN Staff, 17 January 2008, ComputerDealerNews.com.

[2] "Catch Me If You Can: The True Story of a Real Fake," Frank W. Abagnale and Stan Redding, August 2000, Broadway Books.

[3] *Catch Me If You Can*, Directed by Steven Spielberg, DreamWorks, 2002.

22

Case Two – Cain

The second case of firing happens in the very next chapter in the Bible. Cain, the first son of the first employees, worked in the family business as a day laborer, along with his younger brother, Abel (Genesis 4).

Although Cain tried to please the Boss, his brother got a higher rating during their performance review. When the Boss noticed Cain's displeasure, He offered Cain guidance to help improve his performance, as well as wisdom to protect him from acting out of ill will, but Cain ignored the advice and warning. Instead of responding to admonition with attempts at self-improvement, Cain focused on eliminating the competition, and he did. He killed his brother.

Today, Cain's violence against his brother and co-worker would be considered both domestic and workplace violence, and might influence efforts to enact widespread laws to prevent future similar incidents.

But, Cain's action in his own time elicited an immediate and direct personal response from the Boss. God confronted Cain directly, responded to his sarcasm directly, punished Cain directly, and even protected Cain directly.

This case exemplifies firing with a unique accommodating provision, probably only offered to one person one time in an unusual circumstance. Cain's extreme punishment differed from his father's in that at least his dad still gained something from his toil and they had a place to live, but Cain's included a lifetime of *unfruitful* labor and no stable residence.

"When you work the ground, it will no longer yield its crops for you. You will be a restless wanderer on the earth" (Genesis 4:12).

Although Adam's punishing life of hard, painful work still yielded benefits, Cain faced a lifetime of working without benefit, just all work and no ROI. Plus, his banishment away from God's presence exceeded that of his parents in that Adam and Eve apparently still maintained some communication and communion with God even though He relocated their residential living quarters outside the Garden of Eden. Cain's unique punishment away from God's presence, and Cain's fear about it, prompted the Boss to uniquely respond by providing some sort of lifetime mark of protection and promise of exponential harm to anyone who harmed him.

> *Problem people tend to cause problems, whereas solution people tend to reduce problems by increasing solutions.*

In addition to the special provision offered along with the punishment of firing, this instance highlights circumstances where a disgruntled employee causes another employee harm and accordingly needs to leave the premises.

Bosses do have a responsibility to seek to advise and warn employees, confront them without compromise or taking the bait of distraction, and protect other employees if someone evidences danger. The advantage of free will is that employees have the freedom to respond positively any and every time, whereas the disadvantage is that people also have the freedom to respond negatively, any and every time, if they so choose.

Employees reveal their character when offered advice and/or warning. A person's response to admonition usually spotlights deeper issues quickly. Most poor evaluations do not have extreme results such as the serious injury or death of another employee, but make no mistake, problem people tend to cause problems, whereas solution people tend to reduce problems by increasing solutions, especially when it involves improving themselves.

One may wonder why God did not simply kill Cain in this case to punish him and completely remove the possibility of any future wrongdoing. Maybe the number of people on the planet at the time, God's compassionate character or plans for expansion, or other mitigating factors influenced this interaction. Either way, firing in extreme circumstances may require extreme responses, and may even include a benefit, however undeserved.

Islands Away

Perhaps influenced by Cain's exile from God's presence to the land of Nod, east of Eden, cultures throughout history have exiled criminals and dissidents to remote locations as a form of extreme punishment.

Greeks and Romans utilized local Mediterranean Sea islands, the English sent exiles to penal colonies in Australia and the American colonies, the French sentenced prisoners to the French Guiana Devil's Island and others, the Soviet Union sent exiles to the vast and remote Siberian wilderness region, and the United States confined a total of nearly 1,600 prisoners across a 30-year period from 1934 until 1963 on the rocky Alcatraz Island in the middle of San Francisco Bay.

Famous exiles throughout history include St. John the Apostle's exile to the Aegean Sea island of Patmos, Greece. A 7-mile long, 13-square mile island with 40-miles of coastline and a natural protective harbor, Patmos served as a strategic island on the sea lane from Ephesus to Rome, and included a large administrative center, outlying villages, a hippodrome, and pagan temples. Evidence suggests the Apostle received his revelations on the island, [1] and he may have written the Gospel of John and the Book of Revelation there.

Robben Island, seven miles offshore from Cape Town, South Africa served as a Dutch and British leper colony and hospital for mental patients prior to hosting political prisoners that included former South African presidents Nelson Mandela and Jacob Zuma.

French Emperor, Napoleon Bonaparte, suffered two exiles. He first abdicated his throne in conjunction with the Treaty of Fontainebleau in which the Austrian, Russian, and Prussian allies sent him into exile on the Mediterranean island of Elba in Tuscany, Italy on April 11, 1814. He escaped within the year, returned to Paris, regained supporters, and reclaimed his title in March 1815, only suffer defeat within a Hundred Days at the bloody Battle of Waterloo.

---

[1] Revelation 1:9, "I, John, your brother and companion in the suffering and kingdom and patient endurance that are ours in Jesus, was on the island of Patmos because of the word of God and testimony of Jesus."

His second abdication resulted in his capture and exile by the British to the much more distant southern Atlantic Ocean island of Saint Helena, one of the more remote 47-square-mile area locations on the planet, approximately 1,200 miles west of the African nation of Angola and 1,800 miles east of the South American nation of Brazil. General Bonaparte and 26 accomplices lived in the Longwood House, a six-room former summer residence of the island's lieutenant governor.

> *Though harshly punished, they were allowed select freedoms and provisions.*

Though harshly punished, they were allowed select freedom to read, garden, and enjoy limited outside excursions around the island while under guard. Sir Hudson Lowe, Governor of St Helena, also provided daily supplies that included nearly 90 pounds of meat, 9 chickens, and 17 bottles of wine. While working on his memoirs, Napoleon died in May 1821 at age 52 after five-and-a-half years on the island.

Reflection

Most bosses will never have to fire someone for murder or exile problem people to distant islands. However, extreme circumstances where an employee crosses unacceptable lines that require termination do happen. So may special occasions where an employer mitigates punishment with unusual provision, such an extra amount of severance pay unique to that person and circumstance, an honest letter of recommendation or key phone call that can help provide "safe passage" to a new situation, or even visiting an incarcerated person in prison or helping their family through the difficult times caused by a dismissed employee's infraction(s).

Furthermore, clearly spelling out and explaining terms and conditions up front that can lead to immediate dismissal are extremely important, as well as thinking through various contingency plans should things go awry.

- Does every job contract include terms and conditions related to immediate dismissal for cause?

- Have all employees read them, had them explained by a superior, and signed and dated them as part of their contract?

- Do administrators have practiced contingency plans and protocols for various problem scenarios related to people?

- Are the appropriate inside people, as well as any pertinent outside people, agencies, or authorities aware of any potentially significant problem people?

23
Case Three – Nadab and Abihu

N adab and Abihu were the very first ever employees who were literally fired, and the expression "You're fired!" may have its roots in this flaming incident (Leviticus 9-10).

These two oldest of Aaron's four sons were among the first priests in the newly established tabernacle, and their fiery dismissal occurred their very first official day on the job right in front of everyone. The lead up to the event included the Boss giving their uncle, Moses, detailed instructions on Mt. Sinai about many things, followed by months of the Israelites gathering materials, building the tabernacle and making all the furnishings, detailing the proper protocols for ceremonies and sacrifices, and then preparing the priests and people for opening day festivities.

Aaron and his four sons had just completed a seven-day ordination process. They washed, dressed in special clothes, received anointing, ate special food, and were set apart for priestly service with clearly defined jobs and parameters. They were even commended for their behavior and compliance right beforehand: "Aaron and his sons did everything the Lord commanded through Moses" (Leviticus 8:36).

Imagine opening day ceremonies. After completing months of preparations, the Executive Vice-President and Vice-President of Big Deal go into the sacred place, come out together, bless the people, and then the Boss shows up in spectacular fashion.

> "The glory of the Lord appeared to all the people. Fire came out from the presence of the Lord and consumed the burnt offering and the fat portions on the altar. And when all the people saw it, they shouted for joy and fell facedown" (Leviticus 9:23-24).

Everything seems fantastic! Music, fireworks, feasting, and joyful crowds. Except, apparently, Nadab and Abihu get distracted. They do something unauthorized. They break protocol, right in front of everyone, right in the middle of everything else going well, and right in front of the Big Boss during a climatic special moment on a most special day. These two oldest sons, supposed models of leadership and holiness, headlamps of the way specially selected to serve as examples and teachers to whole nation, boldly commit a sin.

Their misbehavior leads to their immediate firing, blasted into burning crisps, right in front of everyone. The following passage offers strong indications that the boys were probably drunk, and the Boss considered their untoward behavior in the middle of the holy ceremony completely unacceptable.

> "The Lord said to Aaron, "You and your sons are not to drink wine or other fermented drink whenever you go into the tent of meeting, or you will die. This is a lasting ordinance for the generations to come, so that

you can distinguish between the holy and the common, between the unclean and the clean, and so you can teach the Israelites all the decrees the Lord has given them through Moses" (Leviticus 10:8-11).

If the men were merely fringe participants in an office party, a little too tipsy late in the evening after work, a little or even a lot inappropriate in a different place in a different context at a different time, the consequences of their actions might have been different.

However, their infraction occurred on the job on a big day in full view of everyone. They not only diverted attention away from the key person, plan and purpose of the event, their actions publicly corrupted core protocols, and they assumed powers they were not granted.

These employees were fired immediately with no recourse. No chance to apologize, sleep it off, sober up, or regain their senses. Once they crossed the wrong line, poof!

Although this case may seem harsh, leaders do have a responsibility to lead by example. Those in positions of power should exemplify model patterns of behavior.

The error of Nadab and Abihu's ways served as a vivid lesson to all other then present and since future employees. The Boss has rules, important protocols, and exacting standards. This incident clearly revealed that certain violations would not be tolerated, and violators will be prosecuted, perhaps even explosively.

Situations do occur when employees require immediate firing with no recourse. Context matters, and in certain situations, certain contexts, and under certain circumstances, there should be no discussion and no benefits.

In rare cases, an employee or employees deserve public "incineration." Though bosses in civilized societies generally do not physically kill transgressors, a boss may need to fire someone immediately in the act of a public transgression(s), and then use the situation to teach a lesson to others. This is a hard case, and should happen very rarely, if it must happen. However, under certain circumstances, it may be necessary.

Interestingly, in two later incidents Nadab and Abihu's next younger brother, Eleazar, and then Eleazar's son, find themselves involved in publicly punishing transgressing leaders. Eleazar saw what happened to his older brothers, apparently understood the lesson(s), and acted accordingly in later situations.

In one case, the Boss charged Eleazar with cleaning up and making something positive out of the mess that resulted from problem employees (Numbers 16), proving that trouble can lead to triumph.

In another case, Eleazar's son took immediate action when a leader publicly transgressed in collusion with a family member of an enemy leader. While the administration discussed the problem and considered consequences, one of their own did the very thing that caused the problem right in front of everyone. In response to his dramatic and quick response, Eleazar's son received a high commendation for saving the nation, as well as this amazing reward:

"Phinehas son of Eleazar, the son of Aaron, the priest, has turned my anger away from the Israelites. Since he was as zealous for my honor among them as I am, I did not put an end to them in my zeal. Therefore, tell him I am making my covenant of peace with him. He and his descendants will have a covenant of a lasting priesthood, because he was zealous for the honor of his God and made atonement for the Israelites" (Numbers 25:11-13).

Quick and even extreme action may not always be pretty but can result in positive outcomes.

General Resolve

George Washington's strong convictions about authority and accountability began long before the February 1789 Electoral College made him the only unanimously elected chief executive of the United States.

Following Washington's service as a lieutenant colonel in the British Army more than 35 years earlier, Virginia's Governor Robert Dinwiddie appointed the 21-year old a major in command of a thousand soldiers in the first full-time military unit in the colonies.

In an October 11, 1755 letter to his commander-in-chief expressing the "necessity of putting the militia under better Regulation." Washington wrote, "I can confidantly assert that the money expended in Recruiting, Cloathing, Arming, Maintaining, and Subsisting Soldiers who have deserted, has cost the Country an immense Sum, which might have been prevented were we under Restraints, that woud terrifie the Soldrs from such practices."

After Dinwiddie appointed Washington as Colonel and Commander of the Virginia militia forces in 1756, Washington wrote in letter to John Stanwix dated July 15, 1757, "Militia, you will find, Sir, will never answer your expectation — No dependendance is to be placed upon them: They are obstinate and perverse; they are often egged on by the Officers, who lead them to acts of disobedience...the Draughts that were sent from the several counties in this Government, to compleat its Regiment: out of 400 that were received at Fredericksburgh, and at this place, 114 have deserted."

He continued, referring to the 30 deserters apprehended, "I have a Gallows near 40 feet high erected (which has terrified the rest exceedingly) and I am determined, if I can be justified in the proceeding, to hang two or three on it, as an example to others."

Following court-martial proceedings at Fort Loudoun on July 25 and 26, 1757, of the fourteen soldiers the 24-year old Colonel sentenced to death for desertion and insubordination, two were hanged within the week.

These experiences prepared Washington for similar incidents during the eight-year long Revolutionary War between 1775 and 1783, such as the mutiny in January 1781 among about 200 soldiers stationed at Federal Hill in Pompton, New Jersey. Pompton Camp Commander Col. Israel Shreve notified General Washington on Saturday, January 20, "It is with pain that I inform Your Excellency that the troops at this place revolted this evening, and have marched towards Trenton: their behavior and demands are similar to those of the Pennsylvania Line" (who had mutinied a few weeks earlier demanding higher pay and better housing conditions).

Washington replied to Shreve on Sunday, January 21, 1781, "This affair, if possible, must be brought to an issue favourable to subordination, or the army is ruined. I shall therefore immediately march a detachment from these posts to quell the mutineers."

Washington tasked his response to General Robert Howe at West Point on January 22, 1781, "Sir: You are to take the command of the detachment, which has been ordered to march from this post against the mutineers of the Jersey line. You will rendezvous the whole of your command at Ringwood or Pompton as you find best from circumstances. The object of your detachment is to compel the mutineers to unconditional submission, and I am to desire you will grant no terms while they are with arms in their hands in a state of resistance. The manner of executing this I leave to your discretion according to circumstances. If you succeed in compelling the revolted troops to a surrender you will instantly execute a few of the most active and most incendiary leaders." He added, "You will endeavour to collect such of the Jersey troops to your standard as have not followed the pernicious example of their associates, and you will also try to avail yourself of the services of the Militia, representing to them how dangerous to civil liberty the precedent is of armed soldiers dictating terms to their country."

By the next Saturday, January 27th, General Howe's troops overtook the mutineers without a fight, and identified three ringleaders – sergeants David Gilmore, George Grant, and John Tuttle. At Howe's direction, 12 mutineers were forced to form a firing squad and execute Gilmore and Tuttle on the spot. He spared Grant when several soldiers testified that he tried to stop the mutiny.

In a letter to New Jersey Governor William Livingston on January 27, 1781, Washington explained the outcome, "The spirit of mutiny seems now to have completely subsided and to have given place to a genuine repentance."

24

Case Four – Israelite Explorers

A nother case of leadership gone awry occurred among the Israelite representatives selected to explore Canaan. Prior to entering the land promised to Abraham's descendants hundreds of years earlier, twelve men – one from each tribe – were chosen to go spy out the land.

The Boss picked each leader, and Moses commissioned them as representatives of each of their tribes and gave them a clearly defined team task. He added a special request certainly understandable coming from a man traveling in the desert for a couple of years.

> "Go up through the Negev and on into the hill country. See what the land is like and whether the people who live there are strong or weak, few or many. What kind of land do they live in? Is it good or bad? What kind of towns do they live in? Are they unwalled or fortified? How is the soil? Is it fertile or poor? Are there trees in it or not? Do your best to bring back some of the fruit of the land" (Leviticus 13:17-20).

The spies' task involved observation – forward operations in advance of a planned maneuver. The Executive VP expected a detailed report with answers to the specific questions on the project manifest.

However, upon their return, in addition to the requested report, ten of the twelve spies offered an addendum – a negative, unsolicited advisement based on their personal feelings and that were contrary to the Boss's plan. Even though not all the spies agreed, the voicing of their dissonance publicly fostered a rebellion (Numbers 13:26 - 14:10).

Prior to that moment, the whole enterprise stood ready to gain that which had been promised, promised again, and reaffirmed repeatedly, for hundreds of years. Much that the community had endured and experienced over the previous year(s) included preparation for receiving this reward. Imagine an entire corporation poised on the verge of receiving all they had worked for, and then 10 of 12 division managers chicken out and lead their divisions in revolt.

In response, the Boss meted out specific consequences to the ten rebel leaders, specific consequences to all individuals involved, and general consequences that affected the entire organization.

"So, the men Moses had sent to explore the land, who returned and made the whole community grumble against him by spreading a bad report about it – these men who were responsible for spreading the bad report about the land were struck down and died of a plague before the Lord. Of the men who went to explore the land, only Joshua son of Nun and Caleb son of Jephunneh survived" (Numbers 14:36-38).

Every other responsible person, essentially every adult age twenty and up counted in the census in preparation for entering the Promised Land – except for the two honorable leaders – received a lifetime ban from gaining what they rejected the moment it lay within their grasp. The disobedient received a desert death sentence, and their relatives received a punishingly long delay.

This case highlights a firing with specific consequences for the individuals involved, and general consequences that essentially affect everyone else.

The general consequences occurred individually over a prolonged period (nearly 40 years), instead of all together and immediately. The Boss could have just fired everyone twenty and older immediately, and then taken the next generation into the Promised Land shortly thereafter. However, though the older generation caused trouble, they also served the purpose of training up the next generation to be ready to do what they failed to do. This caveat is important. The grumbling adults did not just suffer negative consequences, they also served a positive purpose in the intervening time to mature, season, and train those children who would receive the rewards originally planned for all of them.

Note the issues relevant to representation:

- Leaders are called to higher standards.
- Representatives' actions affect people they represent.
- Individuals are responsible for their own actions, even when influenced by corrupt leaders.
- The actions of a few can negatively affect innocent people.
- Much and many can be destroyed by little.

Just as one person with an ax can sink a ship, one terrorist can destroy many things and people, so can one rogue employee affect a company negatively. Part of living and working in community is that what others do may affect everyone for good or evil simply because everyone shares a common relationship. That element of community is why bosses must think beyond a single circumstance or person. In some cases, firings may include direct consequences to those involved, as well as indirect consequences for others who had nothing to do with an incident.

Oddly enough, imbalances occur when bosses overreact by punishing everyone the same or underreact in such ways that future disobedience is not appropriately discouraged.

Wandering Minstrels

(KLL) An incident involving the transportation of alcohol across state lines and underage drinking occurred during my senior year of high school in conjunction with a long distance, multiple-day marching band competition trip. School leaders expelled key instigators, the band received probation, and the entire school body received a four-year restriction from overnight travel and taking any trips more than a 60-mile radius away.

Like the Israelites, I suppose the four-year punishment allowed everyone involved in the incident in any way to clear the high school system before the prohibition lapsed. However, the incident launched a season of "wandering in the wilderness" that impacted not only who our school played in sports or where our arts groups performed, but also inhibited participation in any advancement in competition that would have required either overnight travel or a trip of more than 60 miles away. The incident's immediate consequences affected those directly involved, and the longer-term consequences affected others who had nothing to do with it simply because we lived in the same community together.

> *What we do is not always about us, and not always about now.*

People in the community still remember the incident decades later. Some former students are now teachers and administrators, many former students have descendants in the school system, and lessons learned from that incident still impact behavior even today.

Present actions can have future repercussions. What we do is not always about us, and not always about now, but can affect people and communities for generations.

25
Case Five – Saul

T he Boss fired the first king over His own nation that He ever hired. Someone that stood out from everyone else in the whole country. Someone anointed through the reigning prominent religious leader. Someone publicly proclaimed as king and designated as the newly developing Israelite nation's political leader – Saul.

The prophet Samuel gave the inaugural king guidance and assistance in a partnership arrangement meant to guide the political and spiritual endeavors of the kingdom.

At one point, the Boss sent a message to Samuel to send Saul on a mission. The prophet shared the Boss's purpose, plan, and clearly defined parameters with the king. However, during the mission, the king decided on his own to revise the Boss's strict instructions (I Samuel 15:9). Even though the change may seem somewhat productive and prudent to an outsider, the king's errant behavior signaled a huge problem.

> Then the word of the Lord came to Samuel: "I regret that I have made Saul king, because he has turned away from me and has not carried out my instructions." Samuel was angry, and he cried out to the Lord all that night (15:10-11).

If God had no claim on Israel, no skin in the game with Saul, and no relevance to the political whims of the nation's king, then Saul's actions meant nothing. However, Saul served as the Boss's political representative; the primary agent tasked with leading the Boss's people the way the Boss wanted them led; and the representative political leader tasked with interacting on behalf of the Boss and in congruence with the Boss with all other nations and political leaders on the planet.

In this case, changing an executive plan in process by opinion, without discussion or prior approval, proved unacceptable, and a sign that the king could not be trusted. The text also indicates that pride and arrogance may have played a role, since Saul apparently left his assigned post to go to the religious center of the kingdom to set up a monument in his own honor (15:12).

When Samuel finally caught up to the king and confronted him, Saul first claimed that he carried out the task exactly as requested. He denied any wrongdoing of any kind (I Samuel 15:13). Upon further examination, the king tried to make excuses and claim that he changed his actions to honor the Boss, not dishonor him (15:15). Then Saul tried to redefine the terms of his contract and claim that everything was fine given the adjustments (15:20-21). Finally, Saul admitted his error, but still tried to blame others and claim honorable intentions. Then, he tried to save face and earn favor (15:24-30).

However, the king's disappointing disobedience, denial, pitiful excuses, fraudulent attempts to redefine, capitulation only under pressure, and feeble attempts to salvage his own exaggerated reputation made his case for him. His actions spoke louder than his words, his detestable disobedience louder than his excuses.

So, the Boss fired Saul, sort of, and rejected his kingship, saying, "You have rejected the word of the Lord, and the Lord has rejected you as king over Israel!" (15:26).

- *Both the Boss and Samuel grieved*: "Samuel left for Ramah, but Saul went up to his home in Gibeah of Saul. Until the day Samuel died, he did not go to see Saul again, though Samuel mourned for him. And the Lord regretted that he had made Saul king over Israel" (15:34-35).

- *Then the Boss told Samuel to anoint a new king*: "How long will you mourn for Saul, since I have rejected him as king over Israel? Fill your horn with oil and be on your way; I am sending you to Jesse of Bethlehem. I have chosen one of his sons to be king" (16:1).

- *In addition, the Boss removed the anointing from the old king*: "Samuel took the horn of oil and anointed (David) in the presence of his brothers, and from that day on the Spirit of the Lord came powerfully upon David. Samuel then went to Ramah. Now the Spirit of the Lord had departed from Saul" (16:13-14).

Interestingly, Saul remained on the job as king for some time, but minus the anointing of his Boss. During the ensuing years of his reign, the wayward king unknowingly hired and trained his replacement (16:15-22). This followed the Boss's plan for making a transition in leadership (i.e. leaving well) that includes training successors. A unique lesson from this case shows that firing people should happen at the appropriate time for the person(s) AND the organization.

Ultimately, Saul reigned for a total of 40 years, but he had no lasting legacy of rulers to occupy the throne and his firing affected his whole family. It also raises this interesting question, "Is a person really fired if they stay on the job and can still cause trouble, especially if they cause trouble for their eventual successor?"

Apparently, in some cases, prudence may mean allowing a fired individual to remain on the job in a functional role of transitional leadership. Typically, transitional leaders span these types of gaps until a replacement arrives. However, the nation of Israel was a young kingdom. Saul had some strengths and David was still young when selected. David literally lived on the edge of death for some time, but the Boss used his experiences to train him and gain him loyal friends who helped strengthen his administration. Youth and inexperience can mature and grow over time, and hardship and hazard can prove as useful for developing a future leader as the heat of a furnace for forging iron and refining gold.

If Saul had proven faithful, one of his sons might have been the wisest and richest man who ever lived (instead of Solomon), and the Messiah might have been called the "son of Saul" (instead of the "son of David"). Yet, history is filled with unfortunate legacies that tarnish what once shone brightly.

Up, and Down

(KLL) Around the year 2000, a well-known executive paid $1 million for naming rights to a YMCA in the suburbs of Houston, Texas. The man served with honors as an officer in the U.S. Navy, earned a Ph.D., and worked as an energy Deputy Under Secretary for the United States Department of Interior. He worked his way up in leadership to serve as president of several companies, finally serving as Chair and CEO of one of the largest energy companies in the world at the time, Enron.

By the end of 2001, Enron's leader had personally sold more than $300 million of his company stock options, much of it right before Enron filed for the biggest bankruptcy in U.S. history up to that point. The company's demise cost more than 20,000 employees their jobs, many lost their life savings, and investors lost billions.

During the summer of 2006, following his conviction for six counts of conspiracy and fraud, Ken Lay asked to have his name removed from the local YMCA, and they complied. Lay died shortly thereafter while vacationing with his family and before sentencing.

Many people that enjoy the facilities today have no knowledge of the benefactor whose gift helped enable their enjoyment, and some that do know are still trying to recover from the personal financial disaster that negatively affected their own families during the ordeal.

Although the fruit of his charitable donation continues to bless many, Lay's name, once etched in stone in honor, even though erased from all evidence on the premises, still evokes ire and causes pain in the minds of many – exactly the opposite legacy he had hoped to leave were it not for different personal and corporate choices.

26

Case Six – Nebuchadnezzar

T he firing of King Nebuchadnezzar stands out for at least two reasons:

1. First, he was not an Israelite king, but the king of a foreign nation – Babylon – an iconic kingdom noted for ungodliness and with a capital city that exemplified much spoken against in scripture.

2. Secondly, the Boss not only fired King Nebuchadnezzar, He also rehired him.

The prophet Daniel recounts the story. Apparently, the king had a strange dream, and Daniel interpreted the dream as a warning from God. When he shared his interpretation, Daniel warned the king of danger and offered a solution.

Daniel initially told the king, "Your Majesty, be pleased to accept my advice: Renounce your sins by doing what is right, and your wickedness by being kind to the oppressed. It may be that then your prosperity will continue."

Twelve months later, while walking on the roof of the royal palace of Babylon, the king said, "Is not this the great Babylon I have built as the royal residence, by my mighty power and for the glory of my majesty?"

Even as he spoke the words, a voice came from heaven, "This is what is decreed for you, King Nebuchadnezzar: Your royal authority has been taken from you. You will be driven away from people and will live with the wild animals; you will eat grass like the ox. Seven times will pass by for you until you acknowledge that the Most High is sovereign over all kingdoms on earth and gives them to anyone he wishes."

Immediately what had been said about Nebuchadnezzar was fulfilled. He was driven away from people and ate grass like an ox. His body was drenched with the dew of heaven until his hair grew like the feathers of an eagle and his nails like the claws of a bird.

Then the king said, "At the end of that time, I, Nebuchadnezzar, raised my eyes toward heaven, and my sanity was restored. Then I praised the Most High; I honored and glorified him who lives forever...My honor and splendor were returned to me for the glory of my kingdom. My advisers and nobles sought me out, and I was restored to my throne and became even greater than before. Now I, Nebuchadnezzar, praise and exalt and glorify the King of heaven, because everything he does is right and all his ways are just. And those who walk in pride he is able to humble" (Daniel 4:27-37).

So, in this case, an employee fails to heed a warning, gets fired for a season, learns his lesson, and then gets rehired. The season includes a removal of the employee's authority and removal from his position. Seven years later, with his sanity restored, Nebuchadezzar's management team reconvenes, and the fired now rehired foreign king rises to greater prominence exhibiting an amazing new attitude.

Sooner Rather Than Goner

Firing is often considered the last word, the final straw. However, sometimes firing for cause may initiate a process that results in positive change toward even greater things.

Consider the case of sportscaster, Dusty Dvoracek,[1] who played in the NFL with the Chicago Bears from 2006-09 and for the Oklahoma Sooners from 2001-05. Dvoracek's college career included two Big 12 championships, two seasons as team captain, winning the Jay Myers Award for Outstanding Freshman Student Athlete and the Sooner Schooner Scholastic Award for Outstanding Student Athlete, and being named to the Academic All-Big 12 Team, the All Big 12, and AP All American teams.

His Sooner career also included getting fired from the team his junior year. The 6-foot-3, 305-pound senior from Lake Dallas, Texas, lost his captaincy and received an indefinite dismissal from the squad by Head Coach Bob Stoops in September 2004 for violating team rules.

"There is a sufficient pattern of behavior to merit Dusty's removal from the team," Stoops said in a university press release. "That is the step we are taking. At the same time, we will continue to offer to Dusty all of the services that are available through our department and the university."

[1] Quotes from Bob Stoops and Dusty Dvoracek were gathered from the following news articles:

- "Dusty Dvoracek defends Bob Stoops after ESPN colleague Paul Finebaum's discipline comments," Staff Reports, 18 April2017, TulsaWorld.com.
- "Got a problem with Joe Mixon? Bob Stoops wants you to meet Dusty Dvoracek," John E. Hoover, 21 July 2015, TulsaWorld.com.
- "Dvoracek kicked off OU team," John E. Hoover and Guerin Emig, 18 September 2004, TulsaWorld.com.
- "Dvoracek gets second chance: OU defensive tackle officially reinstated," Carter Strickland and George Schroeder, 21 January 2005, Athletics Communications, University of Oklahoma.

"I squandered an opportunity to be on a great football team," Dvoracek said, "and embarrassed a number of people, including myself."

Over the next few months, Dvoracek worked to overcome his difficulties, filed an appeal with the Big 12 Conference to be allowed to return to OU, which was denied, and then appealed to the NCAA, which was accepted. His actions impressed Stoops enough that he announced Dvoracek's reinstatement to the team in early 2005.

"I am satisfied that he has earned another opportunity with our program. He paid a penalty in missing most of last season and has impressed me with the way he approached and is approaching his self-improvement," Stoops said.

"It was a hard lesson to learn, but I learned it," Dvoracek said. "The people at OU held me to a high standard before I was considered for a return and I recognize that nobody was required to do this for me. I want to show them that their trust in me is deserved. The only way I can do that is to come back and be the kind of citizen, student and football player that they expect me to be. No amount of talk will do that. It will only be apparent in my actions. I want to leave Oklahoma with a positive legacy."

"Dusty understands the expectations we have for him and the kind of scrutiny he will face in making this return," Stoops explained. "We'll do everything we can to make this a good situation for him, but the choices he makes in personal conduct will ultimately dictate how successful he can be. I believe he is a young man with tremendous potential, both athletically and academically, and I am confident that extending this opportunity for him to finish his career in a positive way is the right thing to do."

More than a decade later, Dvoracek defended the coach who fired him when someone questioned Stoops' record of disciplining players.

"I sit here before you at ESPN, I do a daily radio show for Cumulus radio, because Bob Stoops gave me a second chance," Dvoracek said on air. "I made some mistakes in college. I did some things that I'm not proud of, but he gave me a second opportunity. I know Bob Stoops very well and he's a good man."

Stoops similarly defended the player he once sacked by calling Dvoracek a beacon for others who got into trouble.

"He's a great example of a person that was gone and I was done with him," Stoops said of Dvoracek. "And if he was cast off, who knows what ends up happening to him? As it was, he knew, he changed, he did everything that needed to be done and he's a productive, great citizen now, a family man that does all the right things. And that's what we're to do, is help these young guys grow."

Addressing Issues

Unlike Dvoracek, some people get fired because they are NOT suited for the job, or maybe not that job there and then. Whatever the reason, some people can and do change their attitude, gain more experience, receive more training, or otherwise improve in meaningful ways after getting sacked. Just as Stoops' coaching influence spanned Dvoracek's journey, bosses can play healthy roles in helping people understand the reality of the need to change, as well as engage in helping them improve their circumstances. Leading up to, during, and even after the process of firing, bosses can address a person's issues clearly, concisely, and constructively.

Not everyone will listen, which is one reason many people are ultimately fired, but some may. The shock of losing something can wake people up. Getting fired is one way to bring some people to their senses so they realize that previous supervisory advisements were not just drivel, but actual personal and/or professional issues that needed addressing.

One boss invited an employee into her office to chat. She began by complimenting the employee on something she observed that pleased her. She also asked some questions, including "Why are you here?" "Do you like working here?" "What is your passion?" She sprinkled the discussion with additional compliments about the employee's strengths, gently probed the employee's perspectives relative to various perceived challenges and offered suggestions toward positive resolutions. By the end of the meeting, the two mutually agreed that the employee would no longer return. The employee had wanted to quit anyway but did not want to burn a bridge. The employer allowed for keeping the person if certain things were improved upon, or possibly rehiring later. The employee left graciously with inspiration and guidance, and the employer served a larger purpose beyond her role as an immediate provider of income and work opportunity.

Another business owner recalls that the first person he ever fired responded by threatening to kill him. The intensity of departing exchanges required a physical intervention by another employee, and a call to the sheriff to forestall any additional damaging actions or dangerous altercations. However, two weeks later, the former employee returned to confront his former boss again. His physical presence in the workplace unnerved the owner, and the fired employee's extended hand also confused him.

"I want to thank you," the formerly disgruntled employee said. "Getting fired was the best thing that ever happened to me. It woke me up, and I want you to know that I have already began working on getting my life together. Thank you for being a great boss and helping me get my life back on track."

Like this man, and Dvoracek, and King Nebuchadnezzar, some people do seek to positively address their issues. But, others, including some repeatedly successful people who seem thrive despite not addressing their obvious issues, tend to enjoy success anyway.

Fueled by arrogance and ego, some go through a series of jobs, even getting fired repeatedly, but they never seem to actually pay attention to the personal cause of their termination. Rather, they gather and seek sympathy for the supposed wrongs done to them, blame others, and then do it all over again somewhere else without waking up to reality.

Some bosses are complicit in this, too. They gladly rid themselves of "problem people." They may pass them onward gleefully with no warning comments or offer blithe references without pertinent facts. They do not want to risk being called to account for slander, defamation, or for preventing someone from obtaining a new source of income.

Thus, some serial problem employees may also have a series of enablers that have helped grease the tracks for them. This is not to suggest that any of those employers could have changed the person, or that the employers are ultimately responsible for their released employee's actions elsewhere. However, appropriate and early intervention – as Bob Stoops dutifully provided Dvoracek – as well as truthful sharing with prospective employers seeking reference information, can have positive impacts, including protecting the unsuspecting.

Reflection

(KLL) I once hired a prospect partially based on positive recommendations of at least three previous employers. When I fired the employee later, I reached out to the previous employers again to solicit additional information to help clarify my own understanding of what happened. One of them reacted immediately and almost incredulously.

"You mean you hired that person? Yes, they were that way the whole time they worked for us! I'm surprised the next company hired them, surprised you hired them, and amazed they lasted as long as they did!"

Unfortunately, and confusingly, this was not the same story I heard the first time I spoke with them.

"Why didn't you mention any of that when I called you for a reference?" I asked.

"I was angry, but I also didn't want to ruin their career," he answered. "Plus, they weren't all bad."

However, passing someone along without disciplinary intervention or warning to others represents a genuine disservice to both the former employee and the next employer.

But, I was also complicit in this circumstance. During the interviews, when the employee spoke ill of their former employers. I not only felt compassion and understood some of their feelings, I pridefully assumed I could boss better. What I have learned over time is that if a prospective new employee disses former boss(es) to a future boss, I suspect they may express similar sentiments when the future boss becomes the person's latest former boss.

Certainly, bad bosses and horrible situations exist, but bosses must take care not to be suckered in by unsubstantiated claims. Neither should we succumb to pride when compared positively and glowingly to others getting slammed in contrast. Especially when similar patterns appear among a series of jobs, the most usual common denominator is the employee – and that should raise a wildly waving, bright orange, red or yellow warning flag.

I know someone who once rehired a person who formerly worked for the same organization some years prior. Although the circumstances of the employee's former termination were unclear at the time, based on glowing reports from internal staff, they rehired the former employee. The person did prove of good service for a season the second time around, but several issues arose that – you guessed it – were also issues the first time the person worked there. You might also guess that the staff who offered their glowing recommendations expressed their amazement and surprise that the new boss did not know what they refrained from telling them.

So, after the boss terminated the employee's contract and other prospective employers contacted them for a reference, the boss responded with candor and without malice regarding the person's strengths and challenges, including their history of employment and re-employment at the same place. This honesty and willingness to continue investing in the person's life and success helped the former employee find future employment in jobs better suited to their strengths.

27
Additional Considerations

Circumstantial Discretion

One remarkable opportunity while bossing is that, within reason, many bosses have freedom to exercise circumstantial discretion within their domain. God once explained it this way to the prophet Jeremiah.

> "Like clay in the hand of the potter, so are you in my hand...If at any time I announce (something bad), and if (the one warned) repents, then I will RELENT and not inflict what I had planned. If at another time I announce (something good), and if (the one about to blessed) does evil and does not obey, then I will RECONSIDER the good I had intended" (Jeremiah 18:6-10).

Plans, pronouncements, policies and rules should play the role of servants and not masters. Employee actions and reactions should influence boss responses. An employee's acceptable or unacceptable actions that deserve a certain response can be offset or mitigated in response to an employee's ensuing actions. Sometimes we back ourselves into corners or limit ourselves because we forget that we do have discretion. For example, after Colonel Washington's court-martial proceeds at Fort Loudoun in July 1757, of the fourteen soldiers sentenced to death for desertion and insubordination, Washington used circumstantial discretion to ultimately hang only two men as punishment and warning.

Bosses can tell everybody to go home early, bring someone a special favor just because, or give someone or everyone a reward to celebrate a great accomplishment. Or, bosses can take away something planned or expected due to unruly behavior or inferior performance. Bosses can treat different people in different situations differently. It is one thing to discriminate among equals, and quite another to not do something nice for someone because "then everyone else will expect it." There are differences between favoritism and exercising appropriate circumstantial discretion.

The Scouts

High school junior, honors student, and an Eagle Scout, Brian Agnew, had a knife, ax, and cell phone in his car. A peer glimpsed one of the items in his trunk in the school parking lot and reported the infraction to the principal. According to the Savannah, Georgia school's "Student Code of Conduct" at the time, those items were all banned from school property. The unyielding, zero-tolerance, no-weapons-on-campus response resulted in school officials expelling Agnew, causing an uproar among the community and beyond.[1]

---

[1] "Scout axed from school: Jenkins junior suspended for having knife, ax in car used for scouting activities," Jenel Few, Wednesday, 24 May 2000, SavannahNow.com.

Agnew received an automatic 10-day suspension and had to transfer to an alternative school to finish his junior year. His ban from regular campus activities meant that he missed his spring band concert, National Honors Society Banquet, Honors Night ceremonies, junior prom, two advanced placement exams, and a trip with their band to Washington, D.C. to perform at a White House Bicentennial Celebration.

Skidaway Presbyterian Church pastor, Rev. Todd Collier, commented, "Here's a kid with no record of bad behavior or violence – nothing but stellar performance. He's not walking around like some thug in the hallway. You can't lump them all in the same basket. You've got to handle case by case."

Many suggested administrators should look past the infractions and consider the student's intent and past record before determining punishment. But, local School Police Chief, Ulysses Bryant, insisted that board policies must be followed to maintain order and safety.

"If you're a box boy carrying a box cutter for work, if you have a steak knife in your lunch bag to cut up leftovers, even if you're an Eagle Scout with an ax and knife for scouting, these will not be tolerated."

Similarly, New York High school senior and Eagle Scout, Matthew Walen, received a suspension for having a 2-inch pocketknife locked in a survival kit in his car.[2] And 1st grader and 6-year old Cub Scout, Zachary Christie, received a 45-day suspension and forced enrollment in reform school for eating his lunch with a camping utensil that contained a spoon, fork, bottle opener, and a knife.[3]

---

[2] "New York Eagle Scout Suspended From School for 20 Days for Keeping Pocketknife in Car," Maxim Lott, 13 October 2009. FoxNews.com.

[3] "Boy, 6, Faces Reform School for Carrying Camping Utensil to School," Chris Cuomo, Suzan Clarke and Sarah Netter, 13 October 2009, abcnews.go.com.

In each of these circumstances, a discerning principal or school board, after learning all the facts, could have simply dismissed the incidents with a simple warning. After all, in the not so distant past, many males in communities across America carried knives with them everywhere. Many trucks in school parking lots had gun racks with one or more guns on them on campus nearly every day. Not only that, some current principals and coaches remember times when they used to hunt and even camp on campus with their own principals and coaches before and after school and enjoy some of the most memorable times of their lives.

> *Exercise circumstantial discretion to address different situations differently within reason and for good reason.*

Would dismissing these type incidents in zero-tolerance schools technically violate written policies and rules? Yes.

Would these cases be considered favoritism perhaps positively influenced by a student's known character? Yes.

However, principals and boards, like other types of bosses, should have the power to exercise circumstantial discretion to address different situations differently within reason and for good reason.

Public vs. Private

In any work environment, bosses should assume anything said in private will be repeated in public, and anything said in public will be repeated and discussed at length in private. This is not conjecture, but an observation based on reality. People talk, people need the freedom to talk, and people may need instruction on conversational propriety and impropriety.

God's rationale for sharing information about incidents publicly or privately includes the following:

- "Then all Israel will hear and be afraid, and no one among you will do such an evil thing again" (Deuteronomy 13:11).

- "All the people will hear and be afraid and will not be contemptuous again" (Deuteronomy 17:13).

- "The rest of the people will hear of this and be afraid, and never again will such an evil thing be done among you" (Deuteronomy 19:20).

- "You must purge the evil from among you. All Israel will hear of it and be afraid" (Deuteronomy 21:21).

Warnings and guidance offered include:

- "Hatred stirs up dissension, but love covers over all wrongs" (Proverbs 10:12).

- "Gossip betrays a confidence, but a trustworthy man keeps a secret" (Proverbs 11:13).

- "He who covers over an offense promotes love, but whoever repeats the matter separates close friends" (Proverbs 17:9).

- "Whoever turns a sinner from the error of his way will save him from death and cover over a multitude of sins" (James 5:20).

In general, in the aftermath of a firing, bosses should:

1. Share basic facts.

2. Affirm good and right things.

3. Summarize the problem issues, the consequences, and any helpful lessons.

Out of consideration for fired employees, some bosses opt for silence. One day there, the next day a person is gone with no information shared from the top. No announcement, no party, just an empty chair, cleared out desk, and empty office.

However, attempts at total privacy often backfire because secrecy often encourages gossip. People talk, and in the absence of facts, everyone's inner sleuth awakes from their slumber to solve the latest mystery, and rumors abound. Gossip and rumors may happen anyway to some degree because some people like to share their own opinions as fact even in the face of opposing evidence. However, the pinprick of facts can help keep many situations from ballooning out of proportion.

Bosses should seek to provide prudent and balanced disclosure to the appropriate persons and groups anytime someone is fired. If handled well, the right information shared with the right people will disperse everywhere. Sometimes, information may travel in the form of "Did you hear what happened to so and so?" Other times news may take the form of "Guess who needs prayer and why?" However, make no mistake, the news of someone being fired will often travel fast, both publicly and privately. Bosses do have some power to influence the content and context of the message, and they should take steps to do so with propriety and timeliness.

More Relevant Factors

Consistency and Integrity

Whatever official statements different people make should remain consistent and congruent with the facts of the firing at the time. Trouble comes if parties change their stories, offer different versions, or details do not add up. An agreed upon narrative can be helpful, but only when true and not contrived. Inconsistencies tend to point to deeper truths.

In one of the most notable terminations in history, first century Jewish leaders conspired with Roman authorities to arrest, punish, crucify, and bury the crowd-drawing miracle worker, preacher, teacher, whispered Messiah, shouted "Son of the Most High God," self-described "Son of Man," "Lord of the Sabbath," "Light of the world," "the way and the truth and the life" and only way to the Father, Pharisee and Sanhedrin-labeled "blasphemer" and "criminal," and Roman-labeled "King of the Jews" known to most people ever since as Jesus Christ. The authorities made certain they had the right man, made certain he died as intended, and made certain to secure his dead body in a sealed tomb guarded by trustworthy soldiers. Yet, no one anticipated a violent earthquake, frightful appearance of angels, and awe-inspiring, glorious, physical resurrection of the man after three days.

When the guards told Jewish leaders what happened, they paid the soldiers a large sum of money and requested they tell a different story – the man's friends and followers came and stole his body. However, the man's appearance to more than 500 people over the next few weeks before ascending into the sky with a promise to return bringing rewards and punishments did not jive with the revised, contrived account.

Just as differing perspectives on the true identity of Jesus Christ and whereabouts of his body continue to cause division today, false narratives often increase troubles.

One boss appeared to casually invite an employee to meet him in his office one afternoon. However, upon her arrival, she discovered the meeting also included members of the church's personnel committee. During the short, intense session that followed they dismissed her from her job along with the explanation that they wanted to seek someone older, with more training, and more relevant experience.

Unfortunately, the committee turned around in short order and hired someone younger, with fewer degrees, less experience, and related to a highly favored person within the church. This inconsistency detracted from the supposed honesty and integrity of the committee and the pastor, and confused most people who heard the originally stated reasons and then observed the hiring that followed.

Firings and leadership transitions are usually difficult enough without adding in potentially explosive, poisonous elements such as inconsistency and lack of integrity.

Slander

Both fired and firers tend to slander one another. Neither can control the other after a firing, but former bosses should take care to avoid subversion if they hope to avoid charges of libel and fired employees should seek to avoid sedition if they hope to gain employment elsewhere.

Animosity is a natural supplement for breeding and feeding ugly outcomes, and both parties should refrain from any form of animus or retribution. This warning also extends to former co-workers, who are often tempted to take one side or the other and then wear their opinion like a favorite team jersey on game days. Although propriety is a difficult and fine line to walk, sharing pertinent facts can occur without slander, specifically by avoiding misrepresentation and false charges.

One of the best ways to live this out is to imagine you and the person you are speaking about are in the same room together with all of the important people in both of your lives, including your children who adore you and repeat everything they hear, your grandmothers who think you are wonderful but are still willing to discipline you if you say or do anything to embarrass the family, and God who knows everything everyone has ever said, done, or thought and who will ultimately hold everyone to account. The biblical mandate encourages us to treat others the way we wish they would treat us if we were in their shoes, even if the favor is not returned.

Reflection

(BDM) Over the past decade, I have uniquely viewed digital technology disruption from within as a leader in the world's largest information technology company. Innovations in computing power, process reengineering, and exponential software applications have played a significant role in global marketplace ambiguity, complexity, uncertainty, and raging volatility. We have empowered start-ups in Silicon Valley and elsewhere to compete with Tier 1 players and win. The ability to augment human functions inside large organizations with mobile computers that have more power than those that helped put humans on the moon certainly illustrates creative challengers in the ways we work, especially the intelligent automation of repeatable tasks in finance, manufacturing, and supply chain logistics.

Influenced by global financial market imbalances, both large and small companies have experienced massive work force reductions (WFR). My company fired more than 32,000 of our own employees over several years, and most incidents were none too subtle or abundantly compassionate.

In one case, a division leader called an "All Hands" meeting to inform the entire organization that they were no longer employed by the company and would be escorted off the premises immediately.

In another incident, a manager fired an employee in a private meeting scheduled to intentionally occur immediately after the team's celebration of her 25-year work anniversary.

Conversely, my field-testing of principles outlined in these chapters on firing well brought more positive, even personal results. My assistance to a departing employee in his search for a new job led me to my next assignment. Though not actively pursuing a new role, my wife and I were praying for a job that required less global travel while our children were young. The answer came with the opportunity to organize and build a global team of multi-disciplinary leaders to serve the one of the largest integrated oil and gas companies in the world and providentially headquartered in my home city. I additionally served in leadership for a marketplace missionary organization of nearly 1,000 members in 27 countries across 4 multi-national Fortune 200 companies. I doubt these things would have happened apart from my attempts to employ these principles, reject passivity, accept my own responsibilities, lead courageously, love sacrificially, and invest eternally.

Section Four

Leaving Well

28
Introduction

E verybody leaves. From the organization's founder to the newest arrival, nearly everyone departs at some point for one reason or another. Most bosses do not die on the job. Most are not fired but choose to leave willfully and purposefully. They may retire, move, transfer, receive a promotion, or accept a new opportunity – all of which initiates transition.

The "We Team" Model

This section addresses transitions in leadership from one person in a leadership position to a new person in the same, similar, or a revised position. The insights could apply to anyone in any position, but the focus in this section is on leaders, bosses, and managers. The stated goal – leaving well – is not only admirable, but often critical to maintaining organizational function and consistency in purpose and mission.

Bridging transitions effectively often benefits from a "We Team" instead of a "Me Team" model enhanced when selfless people administer, engage, plan, train, and vision cast from unified group and lifetime-of-the-organization perspectives, not competing I-did-it-my-way agendas.

Relay races provide an excellent analogy for describing successful transitions. A "We Team" of runners carries a single baton, one at a time, each in turn passing one to another in a transition zone before running alone until the next handoff to the next runner. Runners each play a role on their team and teams win or lose races together, with some teams losing dramatically during botched transitions.

The Racers

Leaving well involves the organization, the people left behind, the person leaving, and the new person. Actions by anyone and everyone involved help shape the overall legacy. This is especially true at the end of a person's run. The way one leaves is part of a job just as much as the way one finishes a race is part of the race. Some even say finishing is the most important part of any race.

> *The way one leaves is part of a job just as much as the way one finishes a race is part of the race.*

In one of the more memorable, highly publicized finishing fails, seven-time X-games snowboard cross champion, USA's Lindsey Jacobellis, celebrated a little too early during her event final at the 2006 Winter Olympics in Turin, Italy. Confident in her sizable lead, she added a showboating "method grab" to one of her final jumps but lost her balance when she landed on the edge of her snowboard. She fell within sight of the finish line and Switzerland's Tanja Frieden zoomed past her to take the gold medal.

"I was caught up in the moment, "Jacobellis admitted. "I think every now and then you might see something like that. I didn't even think twice. I was having fun and that's what snowboarding is. I was ahead. I wanted to share with the crowd my enthusiasm. I messed up. It happens."[1]

University of Minnesota's Heather Dorniden's 600-meter race in the 2008 Big Ten Indoor Championship similarly received much publicity. Unlike Jacobellis, Dorniden won, but not before falling flat on her face in the second lap. She then astounded everyone by coming from last place to first place during the third and final lap, an extraordinary effort that helped her team clinch the championship.

"After I fell, it was as if a vacuum had sucked all the energy out of the place," Dorniden recalls thinking. "Then, as I started to gain momentum, it was like a crescendo of noise and excitement, all the way to the finish line...I knew the point scores were close for the team championship, so all I really thought was I need to keep running, because if I finish I'll at least earn one point."[2]

In another race claimed by many at the time as the greatest track performance anyone had ever seen, Scotsman and missionary Eric H. Liddell similarly achieved victory after an unfortunate tumble. In the race that inspired the 1982 Academy award-winning movie, *Chariots of Fire*,[3] Liddell tripped in a quarter-mile race run at Stoke-on-Trent, England in July 1923. His fall put him 30 yards behind the nearest

---

[1] "Sochi Olympics: 10 defining moments," James Masters, 7 February 2014, CNN.com.

[2] "A race to remember: 'I had no idea I fell like that' in inspirational 2008 run," Brent Yarina, 3 June 2015, BTN.com.

[3] *Chariots of Fire*. Directed by Hugh Hudson. Distributed by Warner Bros. (USA & Canada) and 20th Century Fox (International), 1981.

runner, but with fierce determination, he overtook the leader three yards before the finish line for the win.

Asked his strategy for running a 400-meter race, Liddell replied, "I run the first 200 meters as hard as I can. Then, for the second 200 meters, with God's help, I run harder."[4]

Born to Scottish missionaries serving in China and often accorded the title of first-ever Chinese gold medalist, the Edinburgh University sprinter later beat the world record to claim the gold medal in the 400-meter race in the 1924 Olympics in Paris, France. Billed again as one of the greatest quarter-mile races ever run, his Olympic performance in that event bested his nearest competitor by nearly six yards. During his lifetime, Liddell worked hard at finishing well, and made thrilling history with his efforts.

Relevant Questions

Some jobs serve as stepping stones from one season of life to another. Even a single lifetime career may resemble a stone path made of individual stones spanning youth to retirement. Prospective employers routinely delve into the dynamics of transitions, typically asking "Why?" a candidate left previous jobs. But, consider asking "How" and "What?" questions, too.

- How did you leave previous position(s)?
- How did you finish your best race?
- How did you finish your worst race?
- What did you do right in leaving?
- What did you do wrong in leaving?
- What did you learn in leaving?

---

[4] "Scotland's Greatest Athlete: Eric Liddell Story," by D. Patrick Thomson, 23 June 1970, Research Unit.

One upper-level administrator left a respectable position after a somewhat short term for a more lucrative opportunity. Following his sudden resignation and departure, the former employer discovered that the departing employee left behind almost no physical records of projects and work performed. Other than email attachments and some piles of old personal files clearly left behind as trash, an apparently overlooked flash drive in the desk drawer served as one of the only physical remnants of the administrator's work.

The flash drive files were all copies of job applications and records of interactions with prospective employers whose time and date stamps revealed that they mostly took place during the administrator's employment while supposedly on the clock working for his employer. His often-closed door, private conversations, and secret on and off-site meetings suddenly all made sense and called into question his prior explanations mostly depicted as work-related.

These discoveries not only left project management and resource voids behind, but any respect he enjoyed during his employment waned in the noxious shadow of his exit. The fact that his new employer did not request any reference from the former employer was either an oversight by the new employer, a cunning ploy by the employee to avoid questions, or both.

In another company, an administrative employee found herself faced with the opposite situation. She did not choose to leave, but her boss chose not to renew her contract. Despite the shock, she completed her last months of employment with such diplomacy, grace, and thorough preparation to help her successor that she earned well-deserved praise from her co-workers. Her admirable performance under the emotionally devastating circumstances amazed almost everyone.

Her boss also noticed. Although not well-suited for her soon-to-be previous position, her successful attempts to leave well generated enough favor with her employer that he actively helped her find employment in a job that proved a much better fit for her experience, personality, and skills. Over time, his continuing advice served as a good sounding board to help her explore her work aspirations, and his honest assessments and recommendations shared with prospective and future employers over the years helped them help her continue to advance in her career.

Ultimately, leaving poorly may only confirm why leaving is necessary, or it can sour even fantastic job performances. However, leaving well can memorialize and enhance excellent job performances, and even benefit some who performed poorly while employed.

Three Types of Transitions

The chapters ahead address three common categories of transitions – inside promotion, family succession, and outside hire. You may recall incidents in all three where people left well, and others where things did not end so well. Many situations can go either way.

1. *Inside Promotion*: The transition from Moses as leader to Joshua as leader. An excellent example of leaving well, this review offers relevance to any organization that promotes from within.

2. *Family Succession*: The transition from King David to King Solomon was marked by doing some things well, and other things not so well. This review can

benefit any organization that incorporates familial succession into their leadership model.

3. *Outside Hire*: The transition from the prophet Elijah to the prophet Elisha ("j" comes before "s" is one clever way of remembering them in historical order). This account covers one of the more common transitions among many organizations – hiring persons from outside.

29
Case One – Inside Promotion

F rom a small family clan of 70 people that arrived in Egypt under the protection of one of their own – Joseph, who rose from slavery through prison to second-in-command of all Egypt – the nation of Israel grew exponentially over a period of centuries to include a large multitude of citizens. From among these people, in preparation for a major company relocation, the Boss selected one inside person to promote to the helm and represent the Owner.

Moses, living in exile in another country at the time, did not apply for a company position, and certainly not THAT position. Moses did not even seem to recognize God during their initial interactions, and the offer of executive leadership elicited both surprise and reluctance from the candidate.

However, God's handpicked CEO then served for four decades. Those forty years of unique distinction basically represented a lifetime appointment that only formally ended with his death. Who can follow that? Who would want to?

This chapter explores various transition preparations that happened during Moses' leadership, at the end of his season in his position, and afterwards. Specifically, how did the Boss help prepare Moses to leave well? How did the Boss prepare a successor? How did that transition begin, and how did it play out over time?

Moses Leading

Working as an Owner's Representative to accomplish God's purposes, Moses served as agent, intermediary, judge, executive leader, and voice to the people. The Boss observed, listened, and acted through and in conjunction with the CEO that He helped train and equip, and who served mostly obediently and faithfully. Moses and his Boss worked together through a top-level executive team that included Moses, his brother Aaron, and their sister Miriam. Additional leadership included the following:

- *Tribal leaders* – "One man from each tribe, each the head of his family, is to help you" (Numbers 1:4).

- *The 70 Elders* – anointed by the Spirit to help carry the burden of leadership (Numbers 1:10-30).

- *The commanders* – wise, respected leaders appointed in authority over groups of one thousand, one hundred, fifty, and tens (Deuteronomy 1:9-17).

Joshua Learning

Moses' successor first appears as a valiant soldier shortly after the nation's exodus from Egypt. A local tribe, afraid of the approaching horde of people, attacks Israel. Moses asks Joshua to lead the battle, and Joshua successfully leads a fight against the Amalekites.

Interestingly, during Joshua's first appearance, the executive team of Moses, Aaron, and Hur (possibly Miriam's husband) watch the battle from the top of a hill. As long as Moses holds his hands up, the momentum of the battle favors the Israelites, but whenever Moses drops his hands down to his side, the momentum favors the Amalekites. The leadership solution they implement in this instance involves admirable teamwork. While Joshua leads the fighting on the battlefield, Aaron and Hur position themselves on either side of Moses and hold up his arms for him. Together, they not only prevail and overcome the Amalekite army, they help make each other successful (Exodus 17:8-15).

Thereafter, Joshua, appears repeatedly as an aide to the executive leader, Moses. Via this apprenticeship, Joshua learns principles of leadership up close and personal.

- *Joshua appears with Moses on Mt. Sinai*
  - Moses sets out with Joshua as his aide and goes up the mountain of God (Exodus 24:13).
  - Moses tells the elders, "Wait here for us until we come back" (Exodus 24:14).
  - Moses (and seemingly Joshua) spend 40 days/40 nights on the mountain (Exodus 32:18).
  - Joshua says to Moses on the way back down the mountain, "There is the sound of war in the camp..." (Exodus 32:17).

- *Joshua appears with Moses in the Tent of Meeting*
  - Moses pitches a tent outside the camp and God speaks with Moses there.

- o "Moses would return to camp, but his young aide Joshua son Nun did not leave the tent" (Exodus 33:11). This practice of living in the presence of God seems similar to the prophet Samuel's experience growing up in the tabernacle in Shiloh (I Samuel 3).

- *Joshua advises Moses, but his relationship with Moses is neither sycophantic nor pusillanimous*
  - o When the gathered elders manifest the presence of the Spirit of Lord and begin prophesying, two elders missing from the meeting also are filled with the Spirit in their separate location.
  - o When "Joshua son of Nun, who had been Moses' aide since youth" speaks up and asks Moses to stop them, Moses rebukes him (Numbers 11:28).

- *Joshua serves as one of the twelve tribal leaders selected to explore Canaan*
  - o Known as "From the tribe of Ephraim, Hoshea son of Nun," Joshua's name "Hoshea" means "salvation" and his name "Joshua" means, "The Lord saves" (Numbers 13:8).
  - o Joshua and Caleb explore the land for forty days with ten other representative leaders (Numbers 14:6).

- *Joshua honors God*
  - o The consequences of rejecting the original timing and destination of the Boss's relocation plan included punishment by death of every male aged 20+ counted in first census, except Caleb and Joshua (Numbers 14:30 and 26:65).

    o   Unlike the troublemaking ten who explored the land, advised against the Boss's plan, and were punished, Joshua and Caleb received a commendation (14:38) because they "followed wholeheartedly" (32:12).

Notice that all of this happened near the beginning of Moses' reign as leader. Also, although Moses gets most of the attention, Joshua is with and around him most of the time in training, in apprenticeship, and seeing everything from the inside out and outside in for 40 years.

Could this have been intentional? Did the Boss plan this inside promotion in advance and then use all that time and those events for intensive training? Alternatively, did Joshua just prove himself over time to become the obvious choice?

Probably both.

Moses Leaving

As the Israelite period of punishment ends and they begin preparations to enter the Promised Land, Moses gets a private message from the Boss, "Go up and see the land, and then you are going to die" (Numbers 27:12-14). Even though Moses is now 120 years old and apparently still in decent shape, this announcement comes as no surprise. His sister died, and his brother just died. The Promised Land was off limits due to their unfaithfulness at one point. With the nation possibly on their last stop on the wilderness train before arriving at their destination station, it probably made sense to Moses that his wild ride neared an end. So, Moses follows instructions. True to his nature as a protector and shepherd, he also requests a successor. God then responds with a clearly outlined, model transition plan still worthy of utilizing today.

1. **Names, Roles, and Tasks**
   The Boss names a successor and a designated assistant, and clearly defines their roles and tasks. He names Joshua as the new leader, and Eleazar as the new priest designated to help the leader make decisions.

2. **Initiation of Transfer**
   Moses announces his resignation, introduces his replacement, and offers reassurance to the people and his successor (Deuteronomy 31:1-8).

   - *Resignation* – "I am now 120 years old and am no longer able to lead you, and I will not be crossing the Jordan with you."

   - *Replacement* – "Joshua will cross over ahead of you (as your leader)."

   - *Reassurance to the people* – "The Lord your God will cross over ahead of you. He will destroy these nations and you will take possession of their land. Be strong and courageous. Do not be afraid or terrified."

   - *Reassurance to Joshua* – "Moses summoned Joshua and said to him in front of all the Israelites, 'Be strong and courageous. The Lord himself goes before you and will neither leave you nor forsake you. Do not be afraid; do not be discouraged.'"

3. **Commissioning**
   - *Private commissioning* – The Boss conducts a private meeting with Moses and Joshua that includes encouragement, instructions, and warnings (Deuteronomy 31:14-23).

- *Public commissioning* – Joshua is presented before
  Eleazar, who lays hands on him and commissions him
  during a special public service in front of everyone.

4. **Implementation of Transfer**
   - *Shared Authority* – Moses gives Joshua "some" (not
     all, at this point) of his authority "so the whole
     Israelite community will obey him" (Numbers 27:20).

   - *Shared Management* – During contract negotiations
     with several tribes (company divisions), Moses
     outlines the circumstances, conditions, and
     consequences of a contract. He then hands over
     management responsibility to Joshua and Eleazar
     (Numbers 32:1-42).

   - *Shared Tasks* – During the tribal assignments
     apportioning the land, Moses appoints Joshua and
     Eleazar to head up the leadership team that includes
     twelve leaders representing each of the twelve tribes.
     This 14-person commission also includes a
     replacement leader for Joshua, who formerly served
     as his tribe's representative (Numbers 34).

5. **Institution of Transfer**
   Moses climbs Mount Nebo and looks out on what must
   have been a very clear day. God shows him the land from
   north to south and west to the Mediterranean Sea.

   "This is the land I promised on oath to Abraham,
   Isaac and Jacob. I have let you see it with your
   eyes, but you will not cross over into it. (Then)

Moses the servant of the Lord died there in Moab, as the Lord had said. He buried him in Moab, in the valley opposite Beth Peor, but to this day, no one knows where his grave is. Moses was a hundred and twenty years old when he died, yet his eyes were not weak nor his strength gone. The Israelites grieved for Moses in the plains of Moab thirty days, until the time of weeping and mourning was over" (Deuteronomy 34:1-8).

Joshua is then filled with the spirit of wisdom because Moses had laid his hands on him and "the Israelites listened to him and did what the Lord had commanded Moses" (Deuteronomy 34:9).

Joshua Leading

After Moses dies, Joshua becomes the new CEO. The Boss affirms him, encourages him, offers instructions, makes promises, and gives warnings. God specifically reiterates three times, "Be strong and courageous," and adds:

1) Because you will lead these people.

2) Be careful to obey the Book of the Law so you will be prosperous and successful.

3) Do not be afraid or discouraged because I will be with you" (Joshua 1:1-9).

Joshua responds by taking immediate responsibility. He initiates actions, communicates with his leadership team, shares plans, gives instructions, and casts vision. He addresses potential issues head on by reiterating agreements, plans, and promises. The people respond in obedience and mutual encouragement, revealing the practical effectiveness of the transition.

At the beginning of Joshua's leadership, the people said exactly what all bosses love to hear, "Whatever you have commanded us we will do, and wherever you send us we will go. Just as we fully obeyed Moses, so we will obey you. Only may the Lord your God be with you as he was with Moses. Whoever rebels against your word and does not obey it, whatever you may command them, will be put to death. Only be strong and courageous!" (Joshua 1:16-18)

> *Joshua led well because Moses led well, led learning well, and led leaving well.*

At the end of Joshua's leadership, after he dies at age 110 and is buried on his estate in the Promised Land, the author of the end of the Book of Joshua affirms their leader's positive impact by noting that the nation "served the Lord throughout the lifetime of Joshua" (Joshua 24:31).

In summary, Joshua led well because Moses led well, led learning well, and led leaving well. The inside promotion enacted by God, executed by Moses, and employed by Joshua helped successfully bridge a brilliant, successful leadership transition to helm the building of the new nation.

Reflection

(BDM) One of my close colleagues unexpectedly received notice that our company had decided to terminate him from his position. I simultaneously received notice of a promotion – into his position. We both experienced shock and awe and asked ourselves, "Why would God allow this to happen?"

Our ensuing 360-degree journey helped empower us to deeply understand various dimensions related to this type of transition. Our mutually proactive, supportive behavior also benefited our employees and management as they observed us progress through a healthy transition checklist partially derived from the Moses-to-Joshua model outlined in this chapter, with the obvious exception that we had a shorter transition span.

Many witnessed, and questioned, our fortitude to operate on a higher-value plane that honored the decisions of our management team, as well as honored each other and God. We already knew that everybody leaves, we believed in the "We Team" model, and we believed healthy transitions can benefit everyone, even the person leaving. The situation afforded us the opportunity to choose how to live out our knowledge and beliefs when they really counted – when real, up close, and personal.

30
Case Two – Family Succession

S uccessive generations helming family enterprises began early in humanity's history. From Cain following in his father's crop rows to twenty sons of David occupying Judah's throne[1] to fifteen generations of Zildjian's making cymbals, [2] progeny have followed in the occupational footsteps of their ancestors. Like Johnsons in the factory[3] and Grahams in the ministry,[4] transitions from fathers to sons are common, but mantle passing also occurs from parents to daughters, spouse to spouse, and between other relatives.

---

[1] Successive sons of David who served as Kings of Judah include Solomon (king over the united kingdom of Israel and Judah), Rehoboam (the kingdom divided during his reign), Abijah, Asa, Jehoshaphat, Jehoram, Ahaziah, Jehoash, Amaziah, Uzziah, Jotham, Ahaz, Hezekiah, Manasseh, Amnon, Josiah, Jehoahaz, Jehoiakim, Jehoiachin, and Zedekiah.

[2] The oldest family-owned business in America began when Armenian alchemist Avedis Zildjian used an alloy of copper, tin, and silver to create extraordinary clear and powerful cymbals for the Sultan of Constantinople in 1618. The family business relocated from Psamatia, Turkey to America in 1929 and is currently led by fifteenth-generation sisters, Craigie and Debbie. See "About Zildjian" on Zildjian.com.

[3] H. Fisk Johnson is the fifth-generation son to lead S. C. Johnson & Son, Inc. (see SCJohnson.com).

[4] Including evangelists William (Billy) Franklin Graham Jr. (1918-2018), William Franklin Graham III (1952-), and William (Will) Franklin Graham IV (1975-).

This organic apprenticeship model occurs naturally for many but does not necessarily happen easily or effectively. Respectable founders handing over hard-earned empires to family members without the commitment, passion, and skills to manage them make for fascinating legends and movies but leave the type of damage few want for their legacy.

Inappropriate and unsolicited meddling by supposedly retired family leaders can harm organizational health, inhibit current leadership, and even tarnish an admirable legacy. Leaders who fail to leave well can, and sometimes do, cause a multitude of unnecessary problems.

Whether a family owns a business, manages a ministry, or rules an empire, leaving well generally beats leaving poorly and requires thoughtful intentionality.

David's Dynasty

The youngest of eight sons living in the tiny village of Bethlehem near Jerusalem, David received his anointing for kingship while still a young man shepherding his father's sheep (I Samuel 16). Although he apprenticed under a king, his direct heritage included no kings. Thus, David was an outside hire for the top job.

The Davidic dynasty began with David, continued with his and Bathsheba's son, Solomon, and then nineteen more mostly successive sons of David over the next nearly four centuries who ruled as kings of the nation of Judah. The primary aberration occurred when one interloping evil queen mother took over after her son died and she attempted to kill all prospective heirs to secure the throne. But relatives saved an infant grandson and successfully brought him out of hiding and installed him on the throne after six years (II Kings 11).

During his 40-year rule, David sired at least 19 sons by his wives, plus at least one named daughter, and other children by his concubines. Though family succession into the kingship seems to have been presumed, the king did not seem to make either his choice or the transition process clear soon enough to avoid trouble.

Family Infighting

Although the rape of one of David's daughters, Tamar, by his first son, Amnon, infuriated David, the patriarch does not seem to have addressed the incident directly. In the absence of a strong fatherly response, Tamar's brother and David's third son, Absalom, killed the rapist.

Again, David did not address the issue directly. Absalom retreated into banishment for three years before returning home, and even then, could not see his father, the king, for the next two years. The five years of festering led to an attempted coup during which Absalom dishonored his father publicly, set out to kill him, and lost his own life during the battle.

David's second son apparently died early since there is no mention of him other than his name in family lists.

Later, nearing the time of David's death, his fourth son Adonijah set himself up as the new king. However, Solomon's mother and the prophet Nathan intervened to seek clarity from King David regarding his preferred succession plan, since there seemed to be some confusion between the King's private promises to Bathsheba and Adonijah's public actions. When the king fairly quickly and publicly announced Solomon as the new king, Adonijah backed off at the time. However, after their dad died, Adonijah initiated a ploy for Solomon's throne that resulted in his own execution.

Transition

The prophet Samuel directly selected both David and his predecessor, so David did not really have an internal national instance in his own lifetime that modeled how to transition a kingship. Untimely inactions and weak actions complicated the transition, caused trouble for many at the time, and serve as examples of leading and leaving poorly.

However, once the succession plan commenced, David did several things that can conversely serve as healthy models for leaving well. The old king:

- *Privately informed key leaders* of his plans.
- *Publicly commissioned* the new king.
- *Privately instructed* the new king about people, plans, projects, and provisions.
- *Pursued procuring resources and transferring relationships* to help make his successor successful and detailed these in his instructions (II Samuel 12; 1 Kings 1-2; 1 Chronicles 22-26, 28-29).

Then, David left. In his case, he completed the leadership transition by dying. Although common among kingships, and a significant way to procure finality, death is not the only way to leave well.

It Has To Be Good

The J. M. Smucker Company manufacturing and marketing empire began in 1897 when 39-year old Ohio Mennonite dairy farmer, Jerome Monroe Smucker, bought a cider mill and began processing apples from an orchard planted by Johnny Appleseed. He decided to repurpose the by-product apple cider mash to make apple butter using his grandfather's recipe. He hand-signed his name on the paper lid on every half gallon crock and engaged his ten-year old son, Willard, in selling them for 25-cents each out of the back of a wagon.

In the ensuing 120+ years, the Fortune 500 company has grown to include more than 7000 employees netting $7.4 billion in sales in 2017 with an expanded line of many familiar brands of products that include beverages, flours, fruit spreads, ice cream toppings, mixes, oils, pet foods and snacks, sauces, syrups and more.

Willard eventually took the helm from his dad, then Willard's son Paul took over, then Paul's sons Timothy and Richard led the company in various roles, including unique roles as Co-CEO's for a decade. When the family-run business named Timothy's son, Mark Smucker, as the fifth-generation President and CEO in 2016, the reorganization included transitioning outgoing CEO (Richard) to Executive Chairman of the Board and then current Chairman (Timothy) to Chairman Emeritus. Sixth generation Smuckers are already in place engaging in leadership training in harmony with the company's well-defined, long-term strategy.

Smucker progeny do not automatically get to be CEOs but have to earn their leadership privileges. Like Willard, family members often get their first taste of working in the business in their youth, but training also includes getting an advanced degree and working someplace else before working within the Smucker's company portfolio.

According to Gary Oatey, Chair of the Board of Trustee's Nominating and Corporate Governance Committee, the company focuses highly on talent development and operating with a long-term perspective of succession planning. In following the biblical pattern of privately informing key leaders, publicly commissioning new leadership, privately instructing the new leader, and procuring resources and transferring relationships, the transition team highlighted Mark's history of holding senior positions in nearly all of the major businesses within the company over nearly two decades, as well as his consistent record of visionary leadership, innovation, and recognized stewardship of the Smucker company's unique culture. Oatey also noted that the combined shifts in leadership provided for the continuance of strategic oversight and institutional knowledge. [5]

The company claims to define success by more than financial performance, believing that "how" the company does things is as important as "what." These include a strong emphasis on the company's *purpose*; *basic beliefs* of quality, people, ethics, growth, and independence that serve as a basis for strategy, plans, accomplishments, and guideposts for decision-making and daily interactions; and *commitments to each other* of mutual respect that include recognition for a job well done, listening with full attention, looking for good in others, and humor.

"At Smuckers, we have a remarkable team that is committed to developing leaders from within," noted Timothy Smucker, expounding on the family succession model that has served their company so well and may position them as one the few companies to employ a sixth-generation CEO. "Our unique culture is critical to our long-term performance and preserving its strength remains a priority for our Company."[6]

[5] "The J.M. Smucker Company Announces Leadership Transition to Foster Next Chapter of Growth and Success," 7 March 2016, JMSmucker.com.
[6] Ibid.

Moovin' On

The reigning king of chicken restaurants at the time of his death in September 2014 at age 93,[7] Chick-fil-A® CEO Truett Cathy commenced a key executive leadership transition more than a decade before he died. In fact, he initiated the process when his children were young, long before renegade Holstein dairy cows ever appeared.

Dan Cathy, current CEO and former President for more than a decade prior to taking the "grade A top quality" helm, remembers growing up in the business and learning everything inside and out alongside his father. He joined the company officially in 1970 and served for 31 years before his father named him President and CEO in 2001. After that, the elder Cathy stepped back to allow Dan increasing freedom to run the day-to-day operations.

In 2015, Dan announced the highlights of a long-term strategy to continue healthy leadership transitions. The plan involved the promotion of five company employees to the executive leadership team, including Andrew Cathy, Dan's eldest son, thus setting stage for a continuing family legacy at the top-tier level.

In Dan Cathy's announcement detailing the expansion of the team to ten members, he said, "As we position Chick-fil-A® for an even stronger future, we will be strengthened by the wisdom of the leaders who got us here. They are passing the torch to a new generation of leadership who are well prepared to foster growth of a relevant brand in a changing world. They are individuals with character, fortitude, and unparalleled business acumen – our best is yet to come."

---

[7] "The QSR 50 Chicken Segment: The top chicken brands in quick service," 2015 report comparing 2014 sales by QSR®, QSRMagazine.com.

According to Ken Bernhardt, a Chick-fil-A® marketing consultant, "As these people are promoted, the company has a strong enough bench that each of these people have replacements for their previous jobs who are strong and well prepared as they are. More people should focus on people and succession planning as Chick-fil-A does. It pays off big time."[8]

---

[8] Section summary and quotes from press releases, the "About" sections on Chick-fil-a.com, and "Chick-fil-A's executive moves show ongoing focus on internal succession," Maria Saporta, 16 January 2015, SaportaReport.com.

31
Case Three – Outside Hire

U nlike longtime peers and corporate family members who rise to leadership, transitions that involve bringing an unknown outsider in offer different challenges. Often in the case of an outside hire, overlap in leadership is rare. Only after one leader leaves does the other arrive. They may sit in the same seat, perform the same tasks, serve the same functions, and sequentially share the same circle of associates and subordinates, but never meet.

However, God often brought outside people in BEFORE the previous person left. The overlapping pattern occurred with Moses and Joshua, as well as with Saul and David, both successors who enjoyed critical seasons of training and shared experiences prior to the official public transition. The difference is that by the time Joshua and David ascended to the top leadership job, they were no longer outsiders. They served long enough that their selections rank as inside promotions, even though they originally came in from outside the family and tribe of the reigning leaders at the time. Therefore, this chapter explores a situation where the transition period seems much more condensed.

Super Prophet

The prophet Elijah's brief appearances in scripture reveal a spectacular display of God's power working through an individual. Elijah presides over a drought instigated by the Lord as punishment for a disobedient nation led by the evil king, Ahab, and his evil wife, Jezebel. God also works through Elijah to help the destitute through miracle multiplication, to raise the dead, and to initiate an extraordinary "My real God is better than your pseudo gods!" showdown on Mt. Carmel against 450 prophets of Baal and 400 prophets of Asherah.

Elijah's story also provides an inside peek into the mind of an executive who feels lonely at the top and experiences great despair immediately after great victory. His spectacular departure provides a glimpse of the majesty of one of the best exit scenes ever – blazing horses and chariots of fire pick up the retiring honoree and whisk him away into heaven.

Elijah's story provides key wisdom related to leaving well, too, since shortly before his retirement, God directed Elijah to select a successor.

Super-duper Prophet

The Tishbite from Tishbe in Gilead anointed a son of Shaphat from Abel Meholah as his successor. These men were not from the same family, same town, or same tribe. Nor does Elisha seem to even work in the same profession. When Elijah shows up, he sees Elisha plowing with 12-yoke of oxen with he himself driving the twelfth pair. Only a rich farmer could afford that many teams of oxen, and only an owner would initiate slaughtering his own pair and cooking them over fires kindled with his own tools of the trade to celebrate his going away party to start a new career (I Kings 19:16-21).

Yet, this rich man did not immediately assume the top position as super prophet. Rather, he follows Elijah and becomes his attendant. He enters a season of training under Elijah's leadership and example that includes key selection, schooling, serving, and shared experiences.

Although Elijah initiated the transition when he originally anoints Elisha, the actual transition period began with the call, spanned their private and public service together, and ended the day Elijah received his promotion to glory.

Interestingly, many insiders seemed to know about the day of Elijah's promotion BEFORE it happened. Elijah knew, Elisha knew, and so did the companies of prophets at Bethel and Jericho. The outgoing prophet confirmed his imminent departure privately to the incoming prophet on the east side of the Jordan River while 50 men of the company of prophets watched from a distance across the river.

When Elijah asked his successor if he could do anything for him before his ride arrived, Elisha asked to inherit twice Elijah's spirit. This may have meant "I want to be twice as good as you," but could also have meant "You are so awesome and amazing that the only way I can succeed is if I receive twice your giftings." Elijah granted his successor's request on the condition that Elisha must see him leaving.

Sure enough, Elisha and the company of prophets saw Elijah depart. The new man at the top ratified his anointing and succession by publicly performing several miracles. The prophets observed what happened and confirmed, "The spirit of Elijah is resting on Elisha" (II Kings 2:15). The written record of Elisha's ministry after those events go on to describe how he did seem to inherit a double portion of Elijah's spirit and thereby gain his Super-duper Prophet reputation.

Does it seem ludicrous that any predecessor would want their successor to double their success? It certainly does in a "Me" world. But, imagine the amazing missional impact of organizations if double the advancements happened with each transition in leadership.

Training for Change

The Department of Defense (DOD), America's oldest and largest government agency and the world's largest employer, manages over 30 million acres of land with several hundred thousand structures in more than 5,000 different places and employs approximately three million people, including over 1.3 million on active duty, 742,000 civilian personnel, and 826,000 National Guard and Reserve forces.[1] Only the Chinese military People's Liberation Army (2.3 million)[2] and Wal-Mart (2.3 million worldwide)[3] even come close.

So, how does this colossal cooperative with employees in every time zone and every climate around the earth approach transitions? How does the monumental military manage movement and progress? They plan, practice, execute, and evaluate, and do it all over again. They teach, train, and deploy with purpose, passion and the sacrifice needed to "establish justice, insure domestic tranquility, provide for the common defense, promote the general welfare, and secure the blessings of liberty"[4] and "support and defend the Constitution of the United States against all enemies, foreign and domestic."[5]

---

[1] "About the Department of Defense (DOD)," Defense.gov, 1 April 2018.
[2] "The world's 30 biggest employers," 14 September 2017, LoveMoney.com.
[3] "Our Business," Corporate.WalMart.com, 1 April 2018.
[4] Excerpt from the "Preamble to the United States Constitution."
[5] "Oath of Enlistment," Army.mil.

The U.S. Army's repertoire of resources includes the Combined Arms Center's (CAC) Center for Army Leadership *Army Handbook for Leadership Transitions*[6] that stands out as a remarkably practical training reference for effectively and efficiently engaging in many types of leadership transitions.

The CAC synchronizes nearly 40 U.S. Army schools through Army University that educate and train more than 350,000 students annually, including nearly 10,000 students from nearly 90 separate nations and over 10,000 sailors, airmen, and Marines from the Joint Force.[7]

The handbook combines military and civilian practices to offer a direct, organizational and strategic step-by-step guide to help manage the organization's most important resource – people. The detailed action plan flows through six phases summarized as follows:

1. Preparation (Notification to Day 1)
2. First Day
3. Initial Assessment (Days 1-30)
4. Alignment and Team Building (Days 31-60)
5. Establishing Routines (Days 61-90)
6. Sustaining (Days 91+)

"Managing transitions is a leadership responsibility," the handbook explains. "Leader transitions within the Army are significant events for any organization due to their complexity and impacts upon the organization as a whole."[8]

---

[6] *Army Handbook for Leadership Transitions,* U.S. Army Combined Arms Center – Center for Army Leadership, usacac.army.mil.

[7] Excerpted from "What is CAC?" on usacac.army.mil.

[8] Ibid, p. 4.

The final step under *Phase Six: Sustaining* is entitled "Facilitate the Next Transition" and addresses the final necessary action to secure a leadership transition: "What are you doing now to ease the transition of the organization when you leave the leadership position? It's never too early to think about your transition with the incoming leader."[9]

Reflection

(KLL) Some people hate to lose. They will train their children and subordinates to win against others but feel the need to beat them themselves. I trained my daughter to make and manage money, and she surpassed me in both categories. I trained my oldest son to skateboard, and he outperformed me in every area of the sport. I trained my youngest son to play guitar and tennis, and he advanced past me quite quickly in both. In tennis, he beat me with some of most amazing shots ever, skills which he also transferred to win more frequently in table tennis, too.

Yet, in the face of the next generation's rising and surpassing successes, did I feel bad about my performances? Not really. In fact, their increasing mastery and astounding prowess convinced me that I must be a good teacher. Their winning results continue to honor me because even when they beat me, I still win because I taught them. Older generations of our family, along with my wife and I, have helped train, position, and provide for our children in ways that have contributed to their abilities and opportunities to pursue accomplishment and success that honor all of us. When they succeed, the family succeeds with them.

---

9 Ibid, p. 34.

Maybe I just think this way to assuage myself, but I believe the world is a better place when progeny surpass their parents, students supersede their teachers, and successors outperform their predecessors. It is exciting when each person in a team relay runs or swims faster than the previous lap time, when each new leadership team increases company profits and organizational health and strength, and when countries advance under successive administrations. Otherwise, the forward trajectory of the prospective future points downward not upward, and away instead of up, up, and away.

> *Leaving predecessors should do everything possible to help make their arriving successors victorious so that everyone can win.*

Whether transitions involving an outside hire include a direct overlap or not, leaving predecessors should do everything possible to help make their arriving successors victorious so that everyone can win. Some of my successors have reached out to me over the years, and I count it a privilege to continue to invest in *their success* which, ultimately, is *our success* as individuals, *the organization's success* over time within temporal history, and *success under the auspices of God* within His corporate universe. Would that we all serve spectacularly, retire in a blaze of heavenly glory, and those who follow us double our impressiveness!

Epilogue

Leading well is a lifetime journey. The sweep of this book covers thousands of years, a movie credit's length worth of diverse characters, and more potential lessons and practical applications than any reasonable person could remember.

For continuing study on hiring well, managing well, firing well, and leaving well, we encourage you to take advantage of our "Boss Like God" study guides. Designed for individuals, small groups, classes, and large group studies, these resources provide guidance on further exploration of various topics introduced in the book.

We additionally invite you to join our online community for insider access to relevant commentaries and discussions, additional resources, and coordination among various learning communities. To access the study resources, request more information, share your own stories, or contact us, visit our web site at BossLikeGod.com.

About the Authors

Dr. K. Lynn Lewis

(KLL) A seasoned entrepreneur with a diverse professional background in business, education, and ministry, I have worked as an engineer, senior pastor, administrator, director, and CEO, and served in leadership in a variety of organizations and on numerous boards.

I currently serve as President of The Bible Seminary, and am the Founder and President of InspireUSA: *Celebrating the Best of America*®. My productions and publications include articles, books, a cable TV show, dissertation, magazines, musicals, songs, videos, and web sites (for details visit KLynnLewis.com). Books include:

- *Boss like God*, 2018
- *Plight: Revised edition with small group study guide*, 2015
- *Meat and Potatoes for the Soul 2*, 2015
- *Meat and Potatoes for the Soul*, 2013
- *Plight*, 2010
- *The Little Giraffe*, 2010
- *Christian Communication in the Twenty-first Century: Patterns and Principles Relative to the Effective Use of Internet-based Communications*, 2002

After lemonade stands, mowing lawns, and door-to-door candy and broom fundraising sales, my first steady paid job involved working on a farm standing on a five-gallon bucket pounding steel fence posts into the ground with a sledgehammer all day, and then stringing barbed wire fencing across the posts. About the same time, I worked as a surveyor's assistant cutting sight paths four feet high with a machete through woods and bushes and pulling chain over hill and vale to measure distances. Then I worked in a hardware store doing sales, stock, inventory and assembly, even going to people's homes to install appliances, put together bikes, and surprise trampolines at Christmas.

In college, I worked as a free-lance carpenter, non-profit property caretaker, greenhouse construction worker for a large public university, technical researcher for one of my engineering professors, a traveling minister and musician, and served on two church staffs as a youth director.

After college, I worked in civil engineering as an engineer and hydrologist and wrote programming code in a successful quest to computerize our design processes. Then I worked with my wife in student development at a private college, in audio and visual communications during graduate school, then served as a pastor, cable TV preacher, board member and CEO of various non-profit organizations, taught high school and middle school students in a private college-prep school, engaged in cutting-edge research about the emerging Internet with numerous organizations across the country for several years, started an audio-visual and web production and media communications company, worked in development, alumni, fine arts and more in private K-12 education, and have most recently helped launch and lead a graduate theological school.

Though vast and varied, my work and career paths have provided amazing opportunities for adventure, growth, learning, and service beyond my wildest dreams. I believe along the way God used me where I was, but also aimed to prepare me for where He wanted me to be. At this point, I have been mostly continuously employed AND in-training for more than four decades, and I expect both to continue for the rest of my prelude in time in preparation for eternity.

Mr. Beau McBeth

(BDM) As a follower of Jesus Christ, I passionately pursue a life of adventure aligned to my divine calling(s), in covenant marriage, as a committed father, marketplace missionary, mentor, and servant-leader in business management.

My mom planted mustard seeds of faith early in my life, as well as encouraged creative use of my God-given athletic gifts. My dad inspired me academically and provided entrepreneurial inspiration. I had the privilege of earning athletic (tennis) and academic (Lindsay Shaefor) scholarships which enabled me to complete a dual BBA in Marketing and Management Information Systems at Sam Houston State University with honors. I co-founded and sold a successful start-up business while working at a technology incubation venture capital firm. As a continuous learner, professional certifications in Network Engineering and Systems Architecture has led me to an exciting career in a variety of disciplines in emerging technology product development, delivery, strategy, operations, sales, financial stewardship, talent development, and program management at some of the world's largest organizations, including Hewlett Packard, Telstra, and Verizon.

I currently serve as a General Manager for Hewlett Packard Enterprise within Enterprise Top Accounts in the Manufacturing Industries Segment including Robotics and Motion, Oil and Gas, Power Generation and Industrial Automation. I use organizational decision rights to lead a global team of multidisciplinary technologists, service delivery professionals and business managers as we strive to delivery meaningful results for our customers, our company, and ourselves. We focus on bringing together the brightest minds to create breakthrough technology solutions that advance the way our world lives and works. I also serve as Co-Founder of Marketplace Missionaries, as Board Member and Stewardship Director of the Christians@Work Fellowship, and as a mentor for young professional men in discipleship through Cru Houston and Church Project in The Woodlands, Texas.

My purpose is to glorify God by enjoying Him forever, advancing the Kingdom of God on earth while engaging, encouraging, and equipping colleagues to restore workplace vitality through gospel transformation.

I hope we can work together to help accelerate the age of digital augmentation and create the future of work and organizational health through agile workplace experiences using principles outlined in this blueprint for elite workplace performance.